THE UPPER ROOM.

DAILY DEVOTIONAL GUIDE

Sarah Wilke
Publisher

Lynne M. Deming
World Editor

INTERDENOMINATIONAL
INTERNATIONAL
INTERRACIAL

76 EDITIONS
40 LANGUAGES

GN00640815

The Upper Room
September–December 2010
Edited by Susan Hibbins

The Upper Room © BRF 2010
The Bible Reading Fellowship
15 The Chambers, Vineyard, Abingdon OX14 3FE
Tel: 01865 319700; Fax: 01865 319701
Email: enquiries@brf.org.uk
Website: www.brf.org.uk
BRF is a Registered Charity

ISBN 978 1 84101 754 9

Acknowledgments

The New Revised Standard Version of the Bible, Anglicized Edition, copyright © 1989, 1995 by the Division of Christian Education of the National Council of the Churches of Christ in the USA. Used by permission. All rights reserved.

The Holy Bible, New International Version, copyright © 1973, 1978, 1984 by International Bible Society. Used by permission of Hodder & Stoughton Publishers, a member of the Hachette Livre UK Group. All rights reserved. 'NIV' is a registered trademark of International Bible Society. UK trademark number 1448790.

Extracts from the Authorised Version of the Bible (The King James Bible), the rights in which are vested in the Crown, are reproduced by permission of the Crown's Patentee, Cambridge University Press.

Scriptures quoted from the Good News Bible published by The Bible Societies/HarperCollins Publishers Ltd, UK © American Bible Society 1966, 1971, 1976, 1992, used by permission.

Printed in the UK by HSW Print.

The Upper Room: how to use this book

The Upper Room is ideal in helping us spend a quiet time with God each day. Each daily entry is based on a passage of scripture, and is followed by a meditation and prayer. Each person who contributes a meditation to the magazine seeks to relate their experience of God in a way that will help those who use *The Upper Room* every day.

Here are some guidelines to help you make best use of *The Upper Room*:

1. Read the passage of Scripture. It is a good idea to read it more than once, in order to have a fuller understanding of what it is about and what you can learn from it.
2. Read the meditation. How does it relate to your own experience? Can you identify with what the writer has outlined from their own experience or understanding?
3. Pray the written prayer. Think about how you can use it to relate to people you know, or situations that need your prayers today.
4. Think about the contributor who has written the meditation. Some Upper Room users include this person in their prayers for the day.
5. Meditate on the 'Thought for the Day', the 'Link2Life' and the 'Prayer Focus', perhaps using them again as the focus for prayer or direction for action.

Why is it important to have a daily quiet time? Many people will agree that it is the best way of keeping in touch every day with the God who sustains us, and who sends us out to do his will and show his love to the people we encounter each day. Meeting with God in this way reassures us of his presence with us, helps us to discern his will for us and makes us part of his worldwide family of Christian people through our prayers.

I hope that you will be encouraged as you use the magazine regularly as part of your daily devotions, and that God will richly bless you as you read his word and seek to learn more about him.

Susan Hibbins
UK Editor

In Times of/For Help with . . .

Below is a list of entries in this copy of *The Upper Room* relating to situations or emotions with which we may need help:

Anxiety: Sept 24; Oct 2, 24, 28; Nov 15, 21; Dec 10, 11, 14

Assurance: Sept 7, 18; Oct 23; Dec 15, 17, 20, 30

Bible reading: Sept 14, 21, 29; Oct 12, 17; Nov 1, 4, 6, 10

Christian community: Sept 19, 22, 23; Oct 11, 22; Nov 12, 17; Dec 11, 13, 25

Christmas: Nov 28; Dec 1, 4, 5, 6, 8, 11, 23, 24, 25

Compassion: Sept 1, 3; Oct 19; Dec 1, 2, 31

Creation/Nature's beauty: Sept 17; Oct 24, 25, 29; Nov 23; Dec 4, 27

Death/Grief: Sept 10, 18, 23, 29; Oct 13, 23, Dec 1, 2, 27, 30

Evangelism: Nov 7, 9; Dec 9, 11, 16, 18, 24, 28, 31

Family: Sept 5, 9, 20, 27, 30; Oct 1, 2, 6, 8, 12, 17; Nov 21; Dec 8, 11, 16, 22

Fear: Sept 2, 24; Nov 5

Financial concerns: Nov 21, 24; Dec 23

Forgiveness: Nov 27; Dec 8

Friendship: Sept 16, 22; Oct 11, 27; Nov 20; Dec 2, 27

Generosity: Oct 4; Nov 3, Dec 19, 29

God's love: Sept 20, 29; Oct 3, 17, 23, 30; Nov 19, 23, 28; Dec 4, 10, 21, 27

God's presence: Sept 10, 24; Oct 3, 7, 28; Nov 13, 20, 28; Dec 7, 10, 20, 24

God's provision: Oct 2, 16, 19, 21, 25; Nov 8, 18, 25

God's will: Sept 6, 19, 29; Oct 14, 20

Gratitude: Sept 28; Nov 3, 24; Dec 19

Growth: Nov 6, 23

Guidance: Sept 11, 19; Oct 20; Nov 4, 6

Hope: Sept 15, 23; Oct 7, 11, 19

Hospitality: Oct 19; Nov 5, 16; Dec 9

Healing/Illness: Sept 3, 10, 24; Oct 1, 16, 20, 26; Nov 2, 9, 12, 16, 21, 26

Job issues: Sept 6, 15, 22, 23, 27; Oct 21, 28; Nov 8, 21, 24, 30

Living our faith: Sept 1, 15, 28, 30; Oct 2, 6, 13, 27; Nov 9, 27; Dec 16, 18, 31

Loneliness: Sept 29; Oct 19, 22

Loss: Sept 1, 3, 10, 18, 23, 24, 29; Oct 13; Nov 2, 8, 12, 20, 21; Dec 1, 27

Mission/Outreach: Sept 1, 5, 27; Nov 26, 30; Dec 5, 9, 16, 18, 24, 26, 28

New beginnings: Sept 2, 3; Oct 29; Nov 28, 29; Dec 8, 31

Obedience: Sept 1, 6, 17

Parenting: Sept 5, 20, 27, 28; Oct 17, 26, 30; Nov 17, 21, 27; Dec 14, 21

Peace/Unrest: Sept 28; Oct 7, 10, 23, 24

Prayer: Sept 4, 8, 15; Oct 11, 20, 24, 26, 28; Nov 12, 15, 17, 24; Dec 13, 14, 22

Salvation: Oct 10, 15, 22; Nov 29; Dec 3

Serving: Sept 1, 22; Oct 14, 19; Nov 14, 16, 22, 30; Dec 2, 6

Speaking about faith: Sept 9, 27; Oct 22, 27; Nov 1, 7, 26; Dec 5, 12, 16, 28

Social issues: Sept 15; Oct 5, 25; Nov 30, Dec 6, 7, 26, 29

Spiritual gifts: Nov 14, 21, 22, 23, 26

Spiritual practices: Sept 14, 17, 26; Oct 11, 12; Nov 6, 14, 15, 16, 18; Dec 2, 6

Stewardship: Sept 12, 26, 28; Oct 4, 13, 19, 25; Nov 14; Dec 26, 29

Stress: Sept 10, 15; Oct 7, 11, 16; Nov 15, 21, 30; Dec 11

Strength: Sept 24; Oct 1, 16

Tolerance: Sept 25; Oct 1, 5, 10, 23, 24

Trust: Sept 2, 7, 8, 16, 18; Oct 10, 18; Nov 8, 15, 19, 21

Tragedy: Sept 1, 18, 25; Oct 7, 26

'Pray without ceasing' (1 Thessalonians 5:17, NRSV).

My arrival at The Upper Room as its publisher seems a natural step in my journey as a Christian—as if everything has prepared me for this moment.

This ministry grew out of a vision of families reading the Bible and praying together in their homes. I was reared in a household where reading the Bible and prayer were central to our everyday life. Over the years, this little devotional guide has remained a part of our family's daily walk, even as we have scattered across the country and around the globe.

My time in the Peace Corps after college gave me a special appreciation for The Upper Room's international presence. On a deeply personal level, I know the hunger in other cultures for spiritual nourishment and growth, and I'm proud that this devotional guide began reaching out beyond US borders just three years after it started in 1935.

My years as the director of an inner-city mission instilled in me a sense of urgency to share the story of Jesus Christ. This experience also gave me a critical understanding that in order to share it, we must be good stewards of our resources. To strengthen my call to non-profit ministry, I entered business school, and in 2004, a master of business administration degree opened the door to a new career in Christian communication. Today, I'm privileged to join The Upper Room's long line of leaders to ensure the witness of this powerful printed treasure.

Throughout 2010, our 75th anniversary year, thousands upon thousands of you have sent gifts to further the mission of The Upper Room for the future. The magazine was born out of prayer, and in prayer it will continue to thrive. I invite you to pray for me and for this ministry as we find new ways to nurture the vision of helping people spend time with God every day.

Sarah Wilke
Publisher

The Editor writes...

I put a single rosebud in a stem vase and placed it on a small table. After a day the bud was still tightly shut, but towards evening the low rays of the sun reached it, and slowly the petals responded to the light and began to open, showing the beauty of the flower within. The next day I moved the rose nearer to the light, and it continued to open.

The prophet Isaiah once talked about the coming of light, words we associate with Jesus: 'The people who walked in darkness have seen a great light; those who lived in a land of deep darkness—on them light has shined' (Isaiah 9:2, NRSV). Turning forward to John's Gospel, we read again that Jesus' coming into the world is bringing us light; he is described as 'the light of all people' (John 1:4).

Like my rose, we too may have been living in a dark corner where the light cannot reach us. Our past lives and our current circumstances may make us feel that life is full of darkness, and for all sorts of reasons we may think we are stuck there. To accept Jesus as our Saviour, however, means that we do not have to stay in our dark corners. Whatever has held us back, however much of a muddle life has become, the light of Jesus' love can bring us into the light. It may be a slow process. Roses do not open all at once, and life does not change all at once either. But once we are moved into the light of Jesus' love, we will not want to seek the darkness again. Gradually we can 'bloom' into the people Jesus knows we can be.

And in turn, we can bring Jesus' light to others. One of the earliest Christian songs I learned as a child began: 'Jesus bids us shine with a pure, clear light, like a little candle burning in the night'. Looking at the world today, we know it needs Jesus' light as never before. Can you become his light for another person, bringing them too out of their darkness?

Susan Hibbins
Editor of the UK edition

PS: The Bible readings are selected with great care, and we urge you to include the suggested reading in your devotional time.

The One in Need

Read Galatians 6:2–10
Let us not be weary in well doing: for in due season we shall reap, if we faint not.
Galatians 6:9 (KJV)

After a night of pounding rain and howling wind, I awoke to the shrill sound of the telephone ringing. The hurricane had left over two million Gulf Coast residents without electrical power and other necessities of life such as food, water and shelter. Instantly each of us became either a person in need or a person who needed to help.

Ten days later I, who normally live alone, still had ten people staying with me. My daily routine had been tossed aside, and I felt weariness setting in. At that point, God spoke quietly within me. 'Would you rather be the one in need? Imagine their weariness!'

I have concluded that God uses life situations to help us examine ourselves. I had always felt I was a helpful and patient person. But this situation caused me to acknowledge that I needed to grow in my compassion and my willingness to help others. Imagining myself in another person's situation helped me to focus and redirected me to what the Bible tells us God has called us to do. After that, when I felt weary, I remembered that my actions not only help others in a material way but also help others to see God.

Prayer: *Patient and generous God, thank you for the opportunity to serve others. Amen*

Thought for the Day: When we make ourselves available, God uses us.

Link2Life: *Contact your nearest relief organisation and volunteer.*

Queen Ester Martin (Texas)

Igniting Our Faith

Read Matthew 17:14–20

Jesus said, 'Truly I tell you, if you have faith the size of a mustard seed, you will say to this mountain, "Move from here to there," and it will move; and nothing will be impossible for you.'

Matthew 17:20 (NRSV)

Early one afternoon my nine-year-old son asked me to cook hamburgers for dinner. I told him we could have hamburgers cooked on the barbecue, and he was happy because he wanted to help to light the charcoal. After 30 minutes, however, he was frustrated. He said, 'Mum, we won't be eating for ages yet, and I'm hungry.'

I told him, 'Don't worry. All we need is to light a small piece of charcoal to get it going. It won't take long after that.'

Lighting that small piece of charcoal reminded me of a spiritual retreat I had attended. I reflected on all the problems I'd been experiencing that had pulled me away from God, tested my faith and stamped out the hope in my heart. The retreat was the spark I needed to ignite my faith and to confront the difficulties in my life. As a charcoal fire gets its start from a small piece of charcoal, our faith can be ignited by a small but true dose of love and the confidence to trust that God will not abandon us.

Prayer: *Faithful God, grant that in our love for you we will find the spark that ignites our faith. As Jesus taught us, we pray, 'Our Father in heaven, hallowed be your name, your kingdom come, your will be done on earth as it is in heaven. Give us today our daily bread. Forgive us our debts, as we also have forgiven our debtors. And lead us not into temptation, but deliver us from the evil one.'* Amen*

Thought for the Day: Each day, keep alive the flame of hope and faith.

Gabriela Marquez Gomez (Distrito Federal, Mexico)

PRAYER FOCUS: THOSE WHO HAVE LOST THEIR FAITH IN GOD
* Matthew 6:9–13 (NIV)

The Second Chance

Read Ephesians 4:29—5:1

Do not repay anyone evil for evil, but take thought for what is noble in the sight of all.
Romans 12:17 (NRSV)

'It Changed My Life in a Minute' is the name of the workshop I co-ordinate at a hospital in Buenos Aires. When I was 18 years old, an incident happened that changed my life.

One day my school friends and I were waiting at our bus stop. Suddenly, a car jumped a red light and crashed into me. The force of the impact threw me across the pavement and I sustained a severe head injury. I was in hospital for a month, unconscious for most of that time, and my doctors believed I would not survive. But I did survive, and I now walk with the use of special walking canes.

The driver of the car tried everything, including lies, to evade responsibility for the accident or my injuries. I have seen him at various court appearances but at first did not want to look at him. Then I recalled the words of my doctor: 'This girl is a miracle.' I could not waste my miracle being bitter or harbouring thoughts and feelings that would limit my future. And so I began to feel compassion for the offender. 'Because God has given me a second chance at life,' I thought, 'my life should reflect the blessing of that second chance.' Because of that, I have forgiven him.

Prayer: *Giver of life, free us from the hurts we have sustained, and help us to repair the harm we have caused others. We are grateful that you forgive us. Amen*

Thought for the Day: Learning to forgive frees us to move forward in spite of our losses.

Paula Tresols (Buenos Aires, Argentina)

Intercessory Prayer

Read 1 Timothy 2:1–6

Let each of you look not to your own interests, but to the interests of others.
Philippians 2:4 (NRSV)

When asked, I find it easy to promise people that I will pray about special needs in their lives. However, keeping that promise is not so easy. Other concerns and activities often get in the way of this most sacred of promises—the promise to lift a person into the channel of God's grace. When I persevere in keeping that promise, I become a link in the chain that includes others who join together as intercessors. But when I neglect to pray, I cheat myself of the privilege of connecting with faithful people who are keeping their sacred promise.

So, to help me remember my promise to pray for others or about particular situations, I carry in my pocket a small, broken link from a chain. Each time I put my hand into that pocket, I can feel the link and choose to be joined with others who are praying. Praying with and for others is a high privilege and holy intimacy that cannot be duplicated.

Prayer: *Loving God, open our ears to the cries of those around us who need your help. Remind us that the call to pray for another is always a holy call. Amen*

Thought for the Day: Praying for others binds us to them with cords of love.

Link2Life: *Create a list of people for whom you will pray regularly.*

John Eyberg (Oklahoma)

Chosen for God's Purposes

Read Jeremiah 1:4–10

The Lord said to Jeremiah, 'Before I formed you in the womb I knew you, before you were born I set you apart.'

Jeremiah 1:5 (NIV)

When you were a child, did you want to hear the story of how you were born? This is the story my mother used to tell me: In 1975 in South Korea, a policeman found me abandoned in a ditch. I was taken to an orphanage, where my adoptive mother later chose me from rows and rows of babies.

I hated the story and never repeated it to anyone. I felt ashamed that I had been abandoned as a new-born baby. I wasn't special enough for my own parents to keep me and not even important enough to leave on someone's doorstep.

Through the joys and heartaches of growing up with my adoptive family, I can now reflect on my humble beginnings and understand that God chose me for my adoptive family. God knew I needed them as much as they needed me.

God often uses people whom the world would not pick to influence others. Moses was 'slow of speech and tongue' (Exodus 4:10, NIV); Jeremiah was 'only a child' (Jeremiah 1:6, NIV); the woman at the well was a social outcast; Rahab was a prostitute. God chooses such people to show us that no matter where we begin, if we allow God to form us and mould us, we can make a difference in the world for God.

Prayer: *Dear God, use us to lead people to you. Amen*

Thought for the Day: No matter who we are or where we come from, God can use us.

Angela Steed (Florida)

Our Life's Work*

Read Matthew 5:1–12

God said to Moses, 'See to it that you make everything according to the pattern shown you on the mountain.'
Hebrews 8:5 (NIV)

Few are called to be leaders like Moses, but all are called to make things; for God who is *our* maker gave us this instinct. How soon we begin with bricks, sand and building-blocks to express this desire!

We were made for full employment. Some make laws; others make ships, cars, homes and gardens. More important, in all our making of things, we are being made ourselves for better or for worse.

Are we consciously working, day by day, in accordance with God's design? In obedience to God's command, Moses rose up early in the morning to be alone with God. The result of his keeping that appointment was the glory of God upon his way and upon his face, and knowledge concerning his life's work.

God had made this world and saw that it was good. We seek, through Christ, to find and to do God's will in all things in this world that God created. In this way, we help to fulfil God's redemptive love and purpose, both in us as individuals and in the world around us.

Prayer: *O God, help us this day to offer ourselves and all our work to your glory. Guide us in all we do, that as you make all things according to your pattern, you may also make our lives into the likeness of Christ. In his name we pray. Amen*

Thought for the Day: When we are dedicated to God's service, our work will bear good fruit.

*To celebrate our 75th Anniversary, we have included this meditation which was originally published on 5 March 1955.

H. Cecil Pawson (England)

Here Today, Here Tomorrow

Read: Psalm 145:1–9
Your kingdom is an everlasting kingdom, and your dominion endures throughout all generations.
Psalm 145:13 (NRSV)

I listened to a group of friends as they talked about rising prices, the lack of jobs and moral decline. I wondered, 'What will life be like for my niece and nephews? What will they face in the coming years?' Fear rose within me. But then I thought of Psalm 145:13.

God isn't a fad—here today, gone in a few weeks or years. The Bible tells us that God was here in the beginning (Genesis 1:1) and will remain beyond the end of time. The same God who walked with the great men and women of the Old Testament still walks among us today and will continue to offer strength and wisdom to future generations. What a comforting thought!

My family coming up in the next generation and their families in the future will face struggles, but they don't have to go it alone. In 2 Samuel 22:31 we read that God 'is a shield for all who take refuge in him' (NRSV). Anyone who looks to God for guidance and 'strength for the battle' will find them provided (Psalm 18:39, NRSV). God's promises are sure, for all time.

Prayer: *God of Abraham and Moses, of all who seek to follow you now and in the days to come, praise your name! You are truly Lord of all, from generation to generation. Amen*

Thought for the Day: From generation to generation, God walks with us.

Connie L. Coppings (Kentucky)

No Request Too Small

Read: Matthew 21:18–22

Pray without ceasing.
1 Thessalonians 5:17 (NRSV)

'You prayed about a lost pen?' my friend exclaimed. I assured her that we did and that we found Bill's treasured pen inside his suit pocket the next day. My friend felt that to pray for something as insignificant as a pen was exploiting God's goodness and mercy. I disagreed with her and explained that we pray about things like lost pens, unexpected dinner guests, rude remarks and all things that are a part of our everyday lives. When our prayers are answered, we celebrate with thanksgiving for God's graciousness. We see God as a member of our family, and God celebrates with us too. When we include God in every aspect of our lives, we feel closeness and intimacy with our Creator.

Jesus told his disciples, 'Whatever you ask for in prayer with faith, you will receive' (Matthew 21:22, NRSV). I well remember whispering my favourite plea the evenings when unexpected dinner guests arrive for dinner and I've prepared food only for the seven in our family. 'Please, Lord, loaves and fishes' (see Mark 6:34–44). God knows what I mean by that prayer, and we have never had guests leave the table hungry.

Whether our prayer requests are large or small, God responds with joy to our trust.

Prayer: *Dear Father, help us understand that you want to be involved in every detail of our lives, no matter how insignificant it may be. Amen*

Thought for the Day: Every part of our day can be an occasion to pray.

Mary E. Dess (California)

Telling the Truth

Read Acts 22:1–16

As it is written, I believed, and therefore have I spoken.
2 Corinthians 4:13 (NRSV)

I joined the church when I was young. I didn't know what being a Christian meant. I was attracted to church activities: singing songs, having overnight prayer meetings and eating goat meat at church gatherings.

Our parents were the first to join a new church in our area, and we followed them. Many people laughed at us because most members of the church were older; it was like the church of old people. Our faith decreased because of how our friends looked at us. When they asked me to what church I belonged or if I still went to that church, I told them lies: 'Oh, I stopped going to that church some time ago.'

One day as I was reading the Bible, I came across the story of Paul. This apostle told people the truth about the life he lived before he knew Christ. Paul spoke with confidence, telling the truth in the presence of a commander and a mob of people, even though people had threatened to kill him. Shame on me for failing to tell the truth to my relatives, who would not harm me!

Speaking about Christ is part of what it means to be Christian.

Prayer: *Thank you, God, for giving us life and for protecting us from harm. You are worthy of praise! Keep us from going in the wrong direction, call to us when we are lost, and lead us in the right direction. In Jesus' name we pray. Amen*

Thought for the Day: Knowing Christ is a privilege to be proud of and to proclaim.

Kondwani Beza (Mzimba, Malawi)

God is Able

Read Psalm 46

God is our shelter and strength, always ready to help in times of trouble.
Psalm 46:1 (GNB)

The doctor's words hit like a punch in the stomach: 'You have Parkinson's Disease.' Of course, this was not what I wanted to hear. Nor did I want to be told a couple of months later that a deadly gene was destroying every organ in my son's body. Within four days he moved from the intensive-care unit to heaven. Months later a beloved aunt was placed in a hospice, to be provided with only palliative care. The night after my aunt's funeral, my mother suffered a massive brain haemorrhage, and the doctors agreed that she could not live without life support. This cluster of losses left me reeling emotionally. Just when I would think I was adjusting, another beloved person would die. This went on for two-and-a-half years.

Recently someone asked, 'What's going to hit your family next?' Frankly, I don't want to know. What I do know is that I am clinging to God's power to help me through these days of grief and sorrow. This power is my hope for the future. At the moment I am weak, but I know that God is strong and is able to carry me through. How do I know? The Bible tells me so. I am supported by God's comforting presence that I experience in loving acts of kindness from God's people.

Prayer: *Thank you, Lord, for carrying us through life's unwanted places. Amen*

Thought for the Day: When I am weak, God demonstrates strength.

Janet Huff (Illinois)

PRAYER FOCUS: THOSE GRIEVING MULTIPLE LOSSES

Learning to Listen

Read 1 Kings 19:1–18
Let everyone be quick to listen, slow to speak, slow to anger.
James 1:19 (NRSV)

For 50 years I have been a licensed amateur (ham) radio operator. Although I enjoy talking with people around the globe, over those years I have probably done more listening than talking. Wanting to hear from as many countries as possible, I would spend hours waiting for a particular international broadcast station. I had to listen patiently for the often-faint sounds of the station in the midst of static and interference from more powerful stations and from some governments that sent out signals to jam certain broadcasts.

I compare this practice of listening to the ham radio to the spiritual practice of discerning God's voice among the often louder voices of the world. When we turn our spiritual 'radio' on, the first thing we have to do is to listen carefully and patiently to ensure that no other station is using the frequency that we have chosen. This reminded me of the words of James in our quoted scripture for today, that everyone should be quick to listen and slow to speak (James 1:19). When I am quick to speak, I am prone to miss what is being said. Listening first enables me to hear the message. When I receive/hear the message meant for me, it helps me to understand what another person is thinking and feeling.

Our God often speaks in a still, quiet voice (1 Kings 19:12) that can easily be missed unless we listen patiently in the midst of life's distractions.

Prayer: *Master, please give us the courage and patience to listen to your voice and also to each other. Amen*

Thought for the Day: Listen for God's quiet voice in loud places.

Ernest S. Lyght (West Virginia)

PRAYER FOCUS: AMATEUR RADIO OPERATORS

So Much More

Read 2 Chronicles 25:1–10

Amaziah said to the man of God, 'But what shall we do about the hundred talents that I have given to the army of Israel?' The man of God answered, 'The Lord is able to give you much more than this.'
2 Chronicles 25:9 (NRSV)

Our house is now worth less than half of what we paid for it. Like many others, we have felt the sting of what is now officially a global economic crisis. We have been working and saving for years, only to discover that what we thought would be our security for our later years is now worth very little.

The Bible shows that relying on human strategies is not new. For example, as a new king, Amaziah faced daunting obstacles, so he bought support to deal with his enemies. Then he felt confident enough to go into battle. But God's prophet explained to Amaziah that winning battles comes not from reliance on armies but from God alone.

I am learning the same lesson. The small advantages we may seem to gain by using earthly means to wage war on our circumstances are nothing compared to what God can give us. Like Amaziah, from time to time many of us want an earthly, tangible and immediate return on our investments. What God promises is intangible and infinitely more valuable. How have you invested your 'hundred talents of silver'? As the prophet said, 'The Lord is able to give you much more than this.'

Prayer: *Dear God, help us to look to the future with confidence in your promises. Through Jesus Christ, our Lord. Amen*

Thought for the Day: What God offers is more certain than anything any human plan could bring us.

Judith Purkiss (London, England)

The Healer of Broken Hearts

Read Luke 4:16–21

Jesus read, 'The Spirit of the Lord is upon me, because he hath anointed me to preach the gospel to the poor; he hath sent me to heal the brokenhearted.'

Luke 4:18 (KJV)

I recently encountered a situation that brought back memories of some past hurtful events. However, I found that I did not feel as hurt as I had back then. In reality, the wrongs others had inflicted on me had done little real harm; nevertheless, those hurtful actions had been very distressing at the time. Commenting to my wife about the past, I said, 'You know, it really doesn't matter any more.'

She replied, 'It really never did', and I responded, 'Yes, I know. But now it doesn't matter to me.' At that moment I realised that God had brought healing to my broken heart.

Wounds of the heart are unique to the person who suffers them. Some hurts we suffer are deeper than others, but every wound affects us. Sometimes the wound doesn't heal quickly. Sometimes we recover without a scar, and sometimes the scar left behind seems never to disappear. Even when others tell us that it shouldn't matter, it may still matter to us. But in every situation, if we turn to Christ, we will find that he still heals broken hearts.

Prayer: *Heavenly Father, help us to move beyond the past and trust you to heal our wounds. Amen*

Thought for the Day: God is in the business of mending broken hearts.

Link2Life: *Decide to let go of one past hurt and forgive the one who hurt you.*

Mark Beaird (Alabama)

PRAYER FOCUS: SOMEONE WHO IS BROKEN-HEARTED

A Lifelong Tradition

Read Deuteronomy 11:18–21

Teach [the Lord's words] to your children, talking about them when you are at home and when you are away, when you lie down and when you rise.

Deuteronomy 11:19 (NRSV)

For most of our 60-year marriage, my husband and I have read *The Upper Room* and our Bible together. Often, we have empathised with a writer's experience and included them in our prayers that day. Each message has enriched our lives.

However, advancing age is taking its toll, and we can't always recall what we read an hour earlier! This upsets us because these devotions are too meaningful to simply allow ourselves to forget. We want to retain what we've read so that we can continue growing closer to God.

We have discovered a solution that is helping us retain the content of the message. Before we begin reading the present day's message, we review the message from the day before. Our sluggish memories begin to 'click in' as we recall the details. This procedure has become important to us. It's based on a principle that we learned in school that constant repetition helps us to retain information. We want to continue to grow mentally and spiritually as long as we have physical life so that we can always be useful to God.

Prayer: *God of all our days, we trust you to be with us as we age. Help us and guide us to take care of ourselves so we can keep alert and serve you as long as we are able. In Jesus' name we pray. Amen*

Thought for the Day: Repetition can be an important key to retaining knowledge.

June Megill (North Carolina)

New Job, New Opportunity

Read Jeremiah 29:1–7

The Lord says, 'Seek the welfare of the city where I have sent you into exile, and pray to the Lord on its behalf, for in its welfare you will find your welfare.'

Jeremiah 29:7 (NRSV)

After losing my job, I knew I had to find new employment to provide for my wife and my son. I finally found a new job in our capital city, a large metropolitan area. My new job also meant I would have to move from my small town to the big city.

During the first two weeks in my job, I felt I had been sent into exile. In the middle of huge traffic jams while taking the bus to work, I remembered my quiet, friendly, small town, where I could go anywhere by bicycle. Then I remembered the Israelites, who were taken into exile by the Babylonians to a foreign country. In the middle of their exile, they received a command from God to remain strong and faithful and to do good work. God told them to seek the welfare of their new city and to pray for the city and its people.

The Israelites' story gave me new insight. God wanted them to seek the welfare of the city where they had been exiled, so surely I should seek the welfare of my new city as well. Anywhere I live I have an opportunity to be God's light of love and hope. And like the Israelites, I can pray for my city and for the people who live in it.

Now as I take the bus to work, I pray for other passengers, the driver and other people on the road. And I ask God to open the hearts of those who need to know Jesus Christ.

Prayer: *Loving God, strengthen us to seek the welfare of those around us. We pray that we can be faithful to all you ask of us. Amen*

Thought for the Day: We find our welfare in seeking it for others.

Bayu Probo (Jakarta, Indonesia)

PRAYER FOCUS: THOSE LOOKING FOR WORK

Friendship and Fellowship

Read Luke 11:5–8

A cheerful look brings joy to the heart.
Proverbs 15:30 (NIV)

From the moment my friend's invitation arrived, I knew it was going to be a special weekend. I was collected from my home in Scarborough on Friday and driven home again on Monday, a round-trip of 160 miles, and a treat I greatly appreciated.

Scarborough Castle melted into the misty distance, and the tyres hummed along the tarmac as we skirted the coast. Our destination was a village wrapped in fields of green velvet as far as the eye could see. At a Christian gathering that afternoon I was presented with a birthday cake and a candle to blow out, and later my group of friends provided a dinner of fish, fresh from the North Sea.

At an all-age service the following morning, in a tiny village church which smelled of ripe fruit, we all enjoyed the fellowship of worship and, afterwards, fruit smoothies. The assorted fruits which went into the blender represented to me the enrichment of God's world through the diversity of his creation.

It was a confirmation of fellowship and friendship in all our lives, a time for refreshment and renewal. It was an outpouring of love. God gives us friends, and that's what friends are for.

Prayer: *We thank you, O Lord, for the love we share with friends. Help us to reach out to those who are friendless, to share your love with them. Amen*

Thought for the Day: Our friendship with God becomes the friendship we share with one another.

Pauline Pullan (North Yorkshire, England)

Garden or Gardener?

Read Matthew 7:24–27

Suppose one of you wants to build a tower. Will he not first sit down and estimate the cost to see if he has enough money to complete it? For if he lays the foundation and is not able to finish it, everyone who sees it will ridicule him, saying, 'This fellow began to build and was not able to finish.'

Luke 14:28–30 (NIV)

I love to grow beautiful, colourful flowers. People have admired my flower garden and have asked me to help them plant a garden. But what I find is that most people really want a gardener. After they have planted the flowers and the hard and tedious work of weeding, watering and pruning begins, many of them neglect the garden. Left on its own, it does not thrive. Having a beautiful, healthy garden comes with a price.

I see a similar pattern in my life. I want to have a close relationship with God and the beauty that a relationship with God brings. But when the hard work of obedience begins, I tend to grow lazy or weary. To have a healthy relationship with God, I must be diligent in the work of tending to that relationship.

Prayer: *Dear God, help us desire to do the work a relationship with you requires so that we grow in obedience to your word. Amen*

Thought for the Day: How am I tending my relationship with God?

Debra K. Johnson (Ohio)

PRAYER FOCUS: GARDENERS

Incomparable Power

Read Isaiah 43:1–7

[God's] incomparably great power for us who believe… is like the working of his mighty strength.
Ephesians 1:19 (NIV)

One week before she was supposed to leave home for college, my daughter, Stacey, was in a serious car accident that left her technically alive but with a body that could not function on its own. Utterly weak and desperate, I questioned God, 'What is your will for Stacey, Lord?' I felt as if I were walking through the valley of the shadow of death alone and blindfolded. 'Please, Lord,' I pleaded, 'I need you to guide me!' After nine weeks on life support, Stacey went home to be with God.

I believe that God answers our prayers, though not always in the way that we hope. In this case, through the support of family and friends and the counsel of clergy and doctors, God gave me the strength to face each struggle. In the midst of despair, I felt comfort and hope knowing that God was with us and was working all things together for our good (Romans 8:28), to give us a hope and a future (Jeremiah 29:11) and that Jesus Christ saves us (see Romans 10:9). Because Stacey trusted in Christ and had a personal relationship with him, I know she is now with her Saviour.

As I trusted in God's goodness, mercy and kindness, I not only survived this great loss; God also strengthened me, restored me and settled my soul.

Prayer: *Dear Father, thank you for the hope you give us through the gift of eternal life in Christ Jesus. In Jesus' name. Amen*

Thought for the Day: I can entrust those I love to God's greater love.

Link2Life: *Reach out to someone who is grieving.*

Nancy Magargle (Pennsylvania)

Signals in the Fog

Read 1 Corinthians 2:6–16

We live by faith, not by sight.

2 Corinthians 5:7 (NIV)

A thick mist or fog sometimes occurs when I play golf in the early morning. We still play in these conditions because we love the game, and usually the fog is temporary. But even though we think we know the golf course well, in the fog it can become confusing and intimidating, and our confidence drains away. Then we hear the players in front of us shout through the fog that the way is clear ahead. Encouraged by the direction of the voice, we play our shots with more confidence. Then when we disappear into the fog we shout in turn to those following us, to direct them to the right path. This help continues until the fog lifts and we can see our way ahead clearly.

How like our Christian journey this is! When we become confused or when we find words of scripture that we don't understand, we need help from our fellow Christians that reassures us, 'This is the way.' We don't give up because we love God, and we know that the mist clouding our way is only temporary. Soon the fog will clear, and once again we will see our way ahead.

Prayer: *Loving God, may we always trust our companions on the journey to help us find the way. Amen*

Thought for the Day: When we are lost, God offers to help us find a way.

Brian Gaunt (East Yorkshire, England)

Treasured Possessions

Read Deuteronomy 7:6–11

The Lord your God has chosen you out of all the peoples on the face of the earth to be his people, his treasured possession.
Deuteronomy 7:6 (NIV)

Just above my kitchen sink is a shelf that holds an interesting collection of treasured possessions. Over the years, my sons, now teenagers, have given me gifts I deeply treasure—a homemade birthday card, a painted flowerpot, a sculpture moulded by hand from clay. These gifts are set apart from other things because they remind me of the special, loving relationship I share with my sons.

Whenever I read the verse quoted above, I think of my kitchen shelf and those treasured gifts and remember that I, like the Israelites long ago, have been set apart as God's treasured possession. Within each of us is a deep longing to be loved and cherished. God loves us not because of who we are or anything we might do. God loves us because love is the nature of God, in whose sight we are of unsurpassable value. No matter where we journey in life, God holds us close and loves us much more than all the earthly treasures we will ever cherish.

Prayer: *Dear God, help us as your dearly loved children to receive all the love and goodness you offer this day. Amen*

Thought for the Day: We are God's cherished possessions, set apart for God's pleasure.

Sandi Marr (Ontario, Canada)

Touching Heart

Read Matthew 13:1–15

Jesus said, 'This people's heart has become calloused; they hardly hear with their ears, and they have closed their eyes. Otherwise they might see with their eyes, hear with their ears, understand with their hearts and turn, and I would heal them.'

Matthew 13:15 (NIV)

I've started playing a guitar again after a lapse of more than 35 years. I haven't played since I was a teenager, and I had forgotten the first major obstacle to playing: tender fingers. Guitar players must build up a layer of calloses on the fingertips so that pressing the strings doesn't hurt.

I finally have a sufficient layer of calloses on my fingertips. But when I pick up a coin, stroke my daughter's hair, or touch my own face, through the calloses I feel only the pressure of an object, not the object itself.

Now I can better understand the barrier between the Lord and me: my heart has become calloused. The Holy Spirit speaks to us within our heart. In right relationship with God, we open our calloused hearts to the presence of the Holy Spirit. If we do, we will not be among those who hear and do not understand, see but are blind, touch but do not feel.

Prayer: *Dear God, forgive us for taking our relationship with you for granted. Soften our hearts and help us to respond to the Holy Spirit. Amen*

Thought for the Day: Living in right relationship with God keeps the heart soft.

Stanley Hurst (Alabama)

PRAYER FOCUS: THOSE WHOSE HEARTS HAVE BECOME CALLOUSED

Time to Love

Read John 15:12–17

No one has greater love than this, to lay down one's life for one's friends.
John 15:13 (NRSV)

For the second time in a week, I received an unusual phone call from a friend. The conversation did not make sense, and I was too busy with work to take the time to dig deeper into why my friend was calling. As I worked through the day my mind kept coming back to the call. Then I received an email reminder from The Upper Room asking for past writers to take time to send in a meditation. All of a sudden it was clear to me: God was speaking to me, just as every morning through the meditations I read in The Upper Room to start my day. I thought, 'How often has some distant writer, many months ago, written something that made a profound difference in my life on the day I read it?'

I realised that I might be able to make a difference for my friend. I stopped what I was doing and phoned him. Soon I learned that he had lost his job and felt too ashamed to ask for help.

God asks us to demonstrate Christian love by taking time in the midst of our busyness to listen and offer love to people in need. Sometimes a few minutes of prayer is all that is needed, but often it is something more. If we routinely abide in God, we will hear God's call each day and know what to do.

Prayer: *O God, help us to abide in you, listen to your call, and demonstrate your love by helping those you bring to us for care. Amen*

Thought for the Day: We are the eyes, ears, voice and hands of God at work in the world.

Link2Life: *Take time to listen in love to those around you.*

Mark H. Anderson (Pennsylvania)

Tradition

Read Hebrews 11:29—12:2
The psalmist wrote, 'I will sing of the Lord's great love forever; with my mouth I will make your faithfulness known through all generations.'
Psalm 89:1 (NIV)

My husband and I are members of a Native American church. As part of our worship service, we sing tribal hymns in our native languages. Even though the words of the songs are familiar, not all of us fully understand them. Nevertheless, a feeling of community and identity speaks deeply to our hearts and our spirits as we sing. Our church is over one hundred years old, and the songs we sing are much older. When we sing these songs in worship, it is as if our ancestors sing with us.

Each year as we experience the loss of more of our elders, we have fewer opportunities to hear tribal languages spoken in our gatherings. Realising that a way of life and being goes with them compounds our grief. Through our songs, we maintain a connection with those who came before us and with the Creator, who promises a great reunion in which all nations will be welcome and all languages will be spoken freely and understood by all. Until that time, our songs remind us that God continues to be faithful to our people throughout the generations. We walk forward in hope, one step at a time.

Prayer: *Creator God, thank you for the many different people who serve you and especially for those who have taught us about you. Amen*

Thought for the Day: Music is a gift that helps us to worship God.

Delana Taylor McNac (Oklahoma)

One Day at a Time

Read: 1 Thessalonians 4:13–18

Do not worry about tomorrow, for tomorrow will bring worries of its own.
Matthew 6:34 (NRSV)

My father was in hospital, critically ill. My husband had just lost his job. My thoughts were consumed with present and future loss. I was broken-hearted when I imagined life without my father and when I thought of my children losing their grandfather. My husband was devastated by the loss of his job, and we feared loss of our income. I wanted to wake up every morning filled with thanksgiving for a new day, but instead I found myself filled with dread and sadness. Not only was I anxious about tomorrow, I was worried about today as well. How could I focus on God's gift of today when I didn't like what today offered?

Sometimes we find ourselves in frightening circumstances. Jesus' words quoted above encourage us not to wish our circumstances away by dreaming about a future time or to make matters worse by worrying about what else might go wrong. Instead, Jesus says that we are to seek the Lord even in the midst of crisis. When we are in sad or overwhelming situations, God promises to be with us. By focusing on today, we discover that God provides the strength and courage we need. We don't have to worry about tomorrow because God will meet us there when tomorrow comes.

Prayer: *God of yesterday, today and tomorrow, be with those who especially need your courage and strength. Amen*

Thought for the Day: Whatever tomorrow brings, God will walk with us through it.

Susan J. Foster (Connecticut)

Extending Hospitality

Read Romans 12:9–13

Welcome one another… just as Christ has welcomed you, for the glory of God.

Romans 15:7 (NRSV)

Our church is a place of traditional worship. We have an older congregation, and because many of our members have died or moved away, our attendance on Sunday was dwindling. The number of children in Sunday school was low, and the church sat unused during the week.

Then the church further down the street burned down. Commonly known as the 'rock-and-roll church' because of its style of worship, it had a much larger congregation than ours. Our minister immediately offered to let the congregation use our church, after our Sunday worship service was over. The members of our church felt apprehensive. Previously, we had rented our church to school groups, with mixed results, and we had lost some of our members because of it.

What a blessing sharing our church has become! On Sunday, with a lot of people in the building, the church seems alive. The two congregations share a fellowship hour between services. I applaud the good work in Christ they are doing in our city. After all, God does not care how people come to know Christ—only that they do.

Prayer: *God of all churches, let us look for opportunities to work together for you. May we show compassion to all those in need. Amen*

Thought for the Day: Most of the differences that matter to us matter not at all to God.

James C. Seymour, Jr. (New York)

Body and Spirit

Read 1 Corinthians 6:17–20

Train yourself in godliness, for, while physical training is of some value, godliness is valuable in every way, holding promise for both the present life and the life to come.
1 Timothy 4:7–8 (NRSV)

All work and no exercise can affect our health. Too little exercise can affect our appearance, endurance, temperament and productivity. Because our bodies are temples of the Holy Spirit, we need to take good care of them.

I have found a way to add exercise to my life. When our public transport fares increased recently in Singapore, I began to get off the bus one or two stops before my destination so that I can exercise and also save some money by walking. The experience is wonderful because I get to see lovely flowers along the way and enjoy a breeze now and then.

We can combine exercising the body and the spirit. This can be as simple as walking alone in the park while listening to a good message or inspiring music, or while praying and interceding for others. Other forms of exercise and activity can take place while we build friendships or mentor a family member or colleague. Exercising with another person who will hold us accountable can help us maintain a disciplined habit of physical activity.

Serving God well involves caring for our body and for our spirit. Both need our daily attention.

Prayer: *Father God, help us to see exercise as a discipline we practise, to stay healthy in body and soul. Amen*

Thought for the Day: Caring for our bodies enables us to serve God better.

Mary Ng (Singapore)

Daily Conversations

Read Isaiah 60:1–3

Choose for yourselves this day whom you will serve… But as for me and my household, we will serve the Lord.
Joshua 24:15 (NIV)

In my role as a director of human resources, I interact with many of the people in the school district where I work. My colleagues and I often engage in conversations about families, holiday plans, significant events and weekend activities. One of my favourite topics is my 12-year-old son and the time we spend together. Another is my church: committee work; worship; volunteering, various projects; and our pastor's humorous, relevant, down-to-earth sermons.

Last Sunday, new members were introduced to and joined our church family. One new member was a colleague who had listened to me talk about church happenings, came to visit and decided to join our congregation. I was honoured to serve as a sponsor for this person. After the service, she immediately came over to me, gave me a hug, thanked me and gave me a gift. What a great feeling it was to see another person find the support of a family of believers!

At times I have wondered about my role in God's family. How can I make a difference? Through God's grace, in my daily life I encounter people who don't know Christ or are looking for a place of fellowship and service. Sometimes conversations provide us with opportunities to lead other people to a life of faith in God.

Prayer: *Dear God, give us words to talk about our faith in daily conversations. Amen*

Thought for the Day: How can I speak up for God?

Link2Life: *Invite someone to church, or prepare a list of three or four ways God has acted in your life and be ready to talk about them.*

Cole Warner (Wisconsin)

Complain! Complain!

Read Philippians 2:14–18

Do everything without complaining.
Philippians 2:14 (NIV)

The queues in the supermarket were long. There were only two tills open, while six others stood unattended. It was the end of the work-day for most of those standing in the queues. Frustration set in, and I stood there and complained like others: 'They should open more tills!'; 'Whatever happened to customer service?'

While relaxing later that evening, I watched the evening news. One of the stories was about a mission in the city that was giving away clothing, shoes and school supplies to children in need. Many homeless and low-income parents had camped out for up to four days on a pavement on behalf of their children. And I had complained about standing 15 minutes in a supermarket queue! What kind of Christian witness did I show to others?

Our patience and peacefulness can shine like a light in a dark and perverse world. Are you shining brightly, or is your light clouded by complaints? Each of us can choose to shine brightly for God.

Prayer: *Heavenly Father, forgive us for complaining, and help us to be patient and show your kindness in difficult situations. In Jesus' name we pray. Amen*

Thought for the Day: For every complaint you make, think of three reasons to be thankful.

Link2Life: *Offer a word of thanks or encouragement to each person who serves you.*

Jacqueline Leaycraft (California)

In God's Arms

Read Psalm 94:14–24

God has said, 'Never will I leave you; never will I forsake you.'
Hebrews 13:5 (NIV)

I had never thought that one day I would live alone, without my dearly loved husband. But it happened; he died young, and I had to get used to new circumstances and to a new focus for my life.

Once when I was feeling especially lonely, I opened my Bible, certain that God would comfort me. I can't remember what passage I read, but I remember feeling as if I were folded in God's arms. I will never forget that loving and tender touch and how I was filled with a joy that only beloved people receive.

We can't ever be truly alone because God offers us a great gift: rich and abundant love. This love is unconditional and endless. Our Saviour is much closer to us than anyone in this world could ever be.

Prayer: *Holy Father, thank you for comforting us when we feel lonely. Help us to feel your presence and to know that you will stay close to us every day. We pray as Jesus taught us, saying, 'Our Father which art in heaven, Hallowed be thy name. Thy kingdom come. Thy will be done, as in heaven, so in earth. Give us day by day our daily bread. And forgive us our sins; for we also forgive every one that is indebted to us. And lead us not into temptation; but deliver us from evil.'* Amen*

Thought for the Day: God offers us comfort that no human can match.

Ivelina Karalambeva (Varna, Bulgaria)

* Luke 11:2-4 (KJV)

Commitment and Example

Read Matthew 10:27–33

Everyone… who acknowledges me before others, I also will acknowledge before my Father in heaven.
Matthew 10:32 (NRSV)

Many Christians pray before meals to thank God for the food they are about to eat. In the comfort of my home this was easy and routine. Yet, for years I did not honour God with prayer before meals in public. I feared being ridiculed for this display of faith. Essentially, every time I ate without giving thanks, I said I was ashamed of being a Christian. I knew this was wrong, and over time my guilt grew.

Finally I made a commitment that I will honour God before every meal, no matter my surroundings. I now pray when I'm alone or with any group of people. All my meals, private or public, start in a prayerful attitude with my head bowed and hands folded as I pray to God.

Recently I led a group of friends in prayer before our meal in a restaurant. Later a man approached me and said, 'Thank you. We used to pray as a family before meals, but we stopped. Your prayer reminded me of what we must do. From now on we will again be praying before our meals.'

Each of us can make a commitment to thank God by praying before every meal. By doing this we honour God and, even though we may never know our influence on others, we will set a much-needed Christian example.

Prayer: *Dear God, let us not be ashamed to act on our faith, no matter where we are. Amen*

Thought for the day: Honour God in all circumstances.

Albert Brooks Drake (Indiana)

Welcoming the Weak

Read 2 Corinthians 12:6–10

Welcome those who are weak in faith, but not for the purpose of quarrelling over opinions.

Romans 14:1 (NRSV)

As someone with fibromyalgia, I tend to think of the term 'weak' as referring to physical struggles. Some days, my hands tremble as I attempt to open jars; my muscles ache when I try to write or brush my hair; and fatigue hangs over my day like a heavy, winter sky. When I'm feeling especially weak, I cling to friends and family who won't tell me that I'm not trying hard enough or become impatient because I'm not as strong as they are. They know I need to feel loved and accepted. And in spite of my slow, wobbly efforts, I still have ways I can share my love with them. I still feel as if I belong.

When I am weak in spirit, I need acceptance even more. We all go through times when our grip on faith is not as tight as we'd like it to be. Yet we still have a place in God's family. Instead of condemning us in our weakness, God welcomes us and leads us to welcome others.

Prayer: *Dear Lord, thank you for welcoming us and using us even when we are weak. Help us not to judge others but to extend your love to those who are weak in faith. Amen*

Thought for the Day: Those around us need welcome more than they need judgment.

Bethany F. Brengan (Kentucky)

PRAYER FOCUS: THOSE LIVING WITH CHRONIC ILLNESS

Richer than My Father?

Read Luke 12:22–34

As for those who in the present age are rich, command them not to be haughty, or to set their hopes on the uncertainty of riches, but rather on God who richly provides us with everything for our enjoyment.
1 Timothy 6:17 (NRSV)

As I hurried along on my morning walk recently, I was visualising my father, who used to stand in the doorway wearing overalls and his crinkled denim cap. Perhaps I should have pictured worry lines on his dark brown face, too, but as I remember him there were none. Daddy knew the secret of living free from worry that Jesus taught us in today's reading.

Worrying would not have changed the meagre income my father made at the sawmill. Our family survived because we didn't have to pay for certain things: we grew most of our own food, and our housing was free because my father worked for our landlord.

Then I found some small coins in the road during that morning walk and instantly thought, 'I'm richer than my father was when I was a child.' Still, while I may have felt richer than my earthly father that morning, I have far greater riches because my heavenly Father shares heaven's riches with me. John 14:2 says, 'In my Father's house are many mansions' (KJV). And I also know Paul's assurance to the Philippians, 'God will meet all your needs according to his glorious riches in Christ Jesus' (Philippians 4:19, NIV). How could I ever need or want more than this?

Prayer: *Generous Provider, thank you for your daily and countless gifts to us. We are grateful for your never-failing love and care. Amen*

Thought for the Day: God cares for us more faithfully and fully than earthly parents ever could.

Jimmie Oliver Fleming (Virginia)

In the Folds of God's Garment*

Read 1 Samuel 25:23–31 and Malachi 3:16—4:3

Abigail said to David, 'Even though someone is pursuing you to take your life, the life of my master will be bound securely in the bundle of the living by the Lord your God.'

1 Samuel 25:29 (NIV)

In Chittagong, Bangladesh, on the other side of the world from my boyhood home, I waited while an old man tugged at the knot in the waist of his lunghi (a one-piece, skirt-like garment for men). It reminded me of my mother's tying a few coins into the corner of my handkerchief when I was a small boy. The old man's gnarled fingers worked until the knot was loosened. Out came some small coins, a tiny box of wooden matches and two old, rusty keys. These were his treasures.

In ancient Palestine the fold of a garment was used in the same fashion. In the verse quoted above, when Abigail blessed David she shared with him a tender picture of God's care. The old man on the streets of Chittagong helped me to understand what Abigail meant and what David understood.

The Revised English Bible makes the picture explicit: 'The Lord your God will wrap your life up and put it with his own treasure.' We are God's treasure, cared for and held close as though we are wrapped in the folds of God's own garment.

PRAYER: *O Lord God, thank you for caring for me. Help me to realise my worth to you and the worth of those around me. Amen*

Thought for the Day: I am one of God's treasures.

* To celebrate our 75th Anniversary, we have included this meditation which was originally published on 8 November 1993.

William D. Barrick (Chittagong, Bangladesh)

PRAYER FOCUS: SOMEONE LACKING A SENSE OF SELF-WORTH

An Endless Stream

Read Matthew 6:1–4

When you help a needy person, do it in such a way that even your closest friend will not know about it. Then it will be a private matter. And your Father, who sees what you do in private, will reward you.
Matthew 6:3–4 (GNB)

Late one evening, while studying in the college library, I overheard a conversation at a table near mine. The mother of one of the students was ill. He wanted to go home to visit her but could not afford to lose the money he would have earned at his part-time job. I was touched by the story and so, quietly, I found out the student's name. Quite sure he did not know me, I looked forward to a chance to do something good in secret.

That afternoon I took the amount he had mentioned from my bank account and folded the money in a piece of paper with these words typed on it: 'Go and see your mother. Love, Jesus.' The money and the letter went in an envelope that I placed in the student's letter-box. It felt good to know that perhaps I had made a difference in the life of the son and his mother.

An endless stream of kindness could flow from each of us to make the world around us a gentler place. Someday when I am in need, the Lord who has seen what I have done in secret may reward me with just the gift I need from a perfect stranger.

Prayer: *Dear Lord, give us eyes to see and ears to hear the needs of others, and grant us cheerful, giving hearts that bring you glory. Amen*

Thought for the Day: God's care and kindness can flow through each of us.

Link2Life: *Do something nice for someone, in secret.*

Anonymous

A Way Among People

Read Colossians 3:11–17

God so loved the world that he gave his one and only Son, that whoever believes in him shall not perish but have eternal life.
John 3:16 (NIV)

The gospel promises abundant, complete life and life beyond death.

God loves the world. God is father of all people and treats us as sons and daughters who need to find the way of life, love, justice, peace, solidarity, reconciliation and companionship.

All of humanity is one family, a community of brothers and sisters whether or not they are neighbours, the same nationality or the same race. God's family today is divided into two hemispheres (the wealthy north and the poorer south); five continents; many social classes, both powerful and powerless; different races and different religions.

The church is a community of people who have known and accepted the love of God and have been challenged to love God and neighbours by overcoming barriers that divide people. The church is a community called to work in partnership with God, announcing God's will that we have life, peace and companionship.

The gospel is the message of God's love and power that invites people to draw to one another and to work for reconciliation, peace and justice. God's love makes the human community one family.

Prayer: *God of love, thank you for the gospel that establishes a network of communion and solidarity, connecting those who are distant and bringing them close to one another. Amen*

Thought for the Day: What can I do to reconcile God's family?

Ronan Boechat de Amorim (Rio de Janeiro, Brazil)

Behind Closed Doors?

Read Luke 12:1–3

Whatever you have said in the dark will be heard in the light, and what you have whispered behind closed doors will be proclaimed from the housetops.

Luke 12:3 (NRSV)

At a rehearsal for my role in a musical I was fitted with a wireless microphone that I was usually careful to turn off when it wasn't needed. However, this particular night I forgot to turn it off. When I returned to my dressing room, the 'private' conversation between another cast member and me was broadcast over the sound system in the auditorium. Everyone heard me criticise a member of the orchestra. I was horrified and deeply embarrassed. My harsh words didn't match the way I want to present myself.

In the reading for today, Jesus tells his disciples of the hypocrisy of the Pharisees who always appeared to be perfect on the outside and who were well respected in the community. But Jesus, seeing their thoughts and knowing even their private conversations, warned that the corruption of their hearts would be exposed.

No matter how good we may look on the outside, God knows the true condition of our hearts and the thoughts behind our words. When we are tempted to criticise or gossip or make unkind comments about someone, we can remember Paul's admonition to 'let [our] speech always be gracious' (Colossians 4:6, NRSV).

Prayer: *Lord of life, create in us clean hearts that reflect your love in all our words and actions. For Jesus' sake. Amen*

Thought for the Day: Today, may all the words I speak be publishable.

Link2Life: *Apologise to someone you've offended.*

Xavia Arndt Sheffield (Maryland)

Under Siege

Read Jeremiah 32:27, 36–41

'I know the plans I have for you,' declares the Lord, 'plans to prosper you and not to harm you, plans to give you hope and a future.'
Jeremiah 29:11 (NIV)

Most of us experience times when we feel as if we are under siege. A close friend of mine is in constant pain and is facing hip replacement surgery. Another has finished a round of chemotherapy and is now beginning radiation to fight her cancer. Another battles debilitating depression.

The prophet Jeremiah spoke to his people who had been literally under siege. The Babylonians had carried them into bondage. But in their suffering, Jeremiah brought a promise of hope and a good future: God has not forgotten them. God promised to 'never stop doing good to them' (Jeremiah 32:40, NIV). Though they would suffer, they would never be alone, never be without hope.

Centuries later, the prophet Jeremiah still speaks to all those who feel as if they are under siege. Disease, war and famine afflict our world. In these and other times of siege, where can we turn for hope? Who can bring peace to our hearts and give us strength to carry on? There is but One, and scripture assures us that nothing is too hard for God. Though difficulty may mark our path, God is stronger and is with us. No matter how hard our struggle, God's promises sustain us.

Prayer: *Dear Lord, help us to remember in times of trouble that nothing is too hard for you. Fill us with your love and with hope. Give us the strength not only to endure but to soar and to see the beauty and the good you bring to us each day. Amen*

Thought for the Day: When we feel besieged, God's love is a strong wall around us.

Lana R. Vannarsdall (Kentucky)

PRAYER FOCUS: THOSE UNDER SIEGE

It'll Be Fun!

Read Romans 8:28–30

Jesus said, 'Happy are those whose greatest desire is to do what God requires; God will satisfy them fully.'
Matthew 5:6 (GNB)

'I don't want to go to school,' my child whined.

'Oh, come on. Perhaps it'll be fun!' I answered hopefully.

Eventually we were in the car and on our way. The complaining continued—then abated. But it resumed as we pulled into the school's driveway.

As I drove away after dropping my child off, the car quiet at last, I wondered about what I had said: 'It'll be fun!' Why do we so often try to encourage one another with 'It'll be fun'? Is the desire for fun our most important motivator? I'm not sure I want to teach children that something has value only if it's fun.

Fun is fine, but is that all there is? What about the thrill of discovery, the pride of accomplishment or the bond of friendship? What about developing social skills, exploring how this amazing world works and exercising both mind and body? What about learning kindness, faith, justice and love of our neighbour? More importantly, what about seeing opportunities to glorify God, to serve with the gifts God gives us? I wonder how we would experience life if we entered each day anticipating the good God is going to do. Perhaps it would be fun. I don't know. But I am sure it would be meaningful, enriching and fulfilling.

Prayer: *O God, we love to have fun. But show us how we can be joyful even when life is not fun. Amen*

Thought for the Day: The goodness of life in Christ goes much deeper than fun.

Brian Hardesty-Crouch (Texas)

Living in the Light

Read 1 John 1:5–10

God is light; in him there is no darkness at all.
1 John 1:5 (NIV)

I love sunshine. The light and the heat make me feel good. One sunny morning I pulled back our bedroom curtains, and unexpectedly part of the curtain rod came out from the wall. Hastily, my husband pushed it back in and said he would mend it properly soon. I told him, 'No hurry.'

Meanwhile the curtains had to stay closed; otherwise the whole rod would fall. Only a thin shaft of light came through the gap where the curtains met. Electric light was a pitiful substitute for the warming, summer sun that blazed outside.

In this dark room I saw a parallel between my feelings of gloom and how I feel when I hold on to unconfessed sin. The world seems a duller place; sin clouds my sense of God's nearness. How I need God's light to give me a sense of well-being! Repairing the curtain rail had not seemed a priority; I thought it could wait. But as the days went by, my room lost its appeal. No longer could I enjoy curling up on the bed with a good book or spending time there with the Lord.

I thought then about how God wants me to deal quickly with any sin that blocks out the light. God encourages me to confess my sin so that I can continue bathing in the light that so brightens my spirit. I'm grateful that I can choose, moment by moment, to live in the light of God's love and forgiveness.

Prayer: *Dear God, shine your light into our life so that all barriers of sin are gone. In Jesus' name. Amen*

Thought for the Day: The light of Christ dispels the darkness in our hearts.

Emma J. Peterson (Surrey, England)

PRAYER FOCUS: THOSE LIVING IN SPIRITUAL DARKNESS

Whom Do You Trust?*

Read Romans 4:13–22

The Lord answered Job… 'Where were you when I laid the foundation of the earth? Tell me, if you have understanding.'
Job 38:1, 4 (NRSV)

All my life I had been a modern-day Pharisee. It was important to me and my security to know what to believe in, what the right doctrine was, which preacher had the 'truth', which church was correct.

In my mind I played a game in which I thought I would be at peace if I figured out the 'truth'. This 'truth' would often change from day to day, but I still played the game—to my own detriment. Finally I heard the voice of God saying to me, 'Why torture yourself? You do not know all the answers, and you never will. I do know the answers, and I can be trusted.'

I did not listen straight away. I kept asking my questions: 'How was the universe made? How can I know the Bible is true?' To every question came the same answer, 'Trust me.'

'But God—' I would say.

'Trust me,' God would answer.

'I need proof!' I would respond.

'You need me,' God would reply.

It is slowly sinking in. No doctrine saves me. Not even the Bible does. God saves me.

Prayer: *Thank you, Father, that I have you. Today I place my trust in you anew, through Jesus Christ our Lord. Amen*

Thought for the Day: Our trust is in the Lord.

* To celebrate our 75th Anniversary, we have included this meditation which was originally published on 21 June 2001.

Tim Burleson (South Carolina)

The 'Upper Room'

Read James 5:13–16

Jesus said, 'Where two or three are gathered in my name, I am there among them.'

Matthew 18:20 (NRSV)

I have a dear friend, Priscilla, whom I haven't seen in the many years since my husband and I moved to a new town. Each morning when I read *The Upper Room* devotional, the title, *The Upper Room*, conjures up fond memories of my friend. It was in the 'upper room' of our church that we met many years ago on a hot, summer evening as we prepared with other church members to teach a holiday Bible class. When asked where we met, Priscilla and I always loved telling people we met in the 'upper room' (Luke 22:12, NIV, KJV).

Over the years as our friendship deepened, our prayer times together grew increasingly precious to me. Priscilla taught me to pray with complete spontaneity. If either of us needed prayer, the next words out of Priscilla's mouth would be, 'Anne, let's pray.' Initially, I would respond, 'Here? Now?' She would always take my hands in hers and begin to pray.

It was important to me for Priscilla to take my hands in hers and say, 'Let's pray.' I felt God's presence in the touching of our hands. I would feel a spark of instantaneous hope, relieving any stress I was experiencing, giving me confidence that God was at work and would remedy whatever the problem was.

Prayer: *Dear Lord, thank you for the gifts of special friends who stand ready to pray for us and for the serenity that prayer gives. In Jesus' name we pray. Amen*

Thought for the Day: When we pray with others, we feel God's touch.

Link2Life: *Volunteer to lead a prayer group in your church.*

Anne Sheffield (Virginia)

Seed Growth

Read Mark 4:26–29 and 1 Corinthians 3:5–9

Neither the one who plants nor the one who waters is anything, but only God who gives the growth.
1 Corinthians 3:7 (NRSV)

I learned about farming from my father who was a cotton farmer. Preparation for the next year's harvest actually starts just as the current year's harvest is complete. As soon as the crops are out of the field, the ground is prepared for the next year's crop to eliminate stalks and preserve ground moisture. The following spring and summer everything is done with precision from selecting seed and the number to be planted per acre to ploughing and planting.

However, regardless of how much preparation takes place, variables always can affect the plan. Insects, hail damage, too little or too much rainfall—all these can increase stress levels for farmers. Even though farmers have a lot of work and planning to do, they cannot make the seed sprout or the plant grow. Only God can do that.

Our spiritual growth is similar. Just as God cannot produce a crop for a farmer who does not plant and tend the field, God cannot grow the fruit of the Holy Spirit in our lives if we do not do our part. Our part involves consistent attention to spiritual disciplines such as Bible study, prayer, worship, putting God first in our lives and caring for those in need. It takes time to grow spiritually, and we cannot make it happen faster. But we can maximise our growth by paying attention every day to the details that are our responsibility.

Prayer: *Dear God, teach us to use the tools you have given us to grow in spiritual maturity. Amen*

Thought for the Day: Spiritual growth is a partnership between us and God.

M. Ted Haynes (Texas)

PRAYER FOCUS: FARMERS

Art in the Dark

Read Psalm 57

I will sing and make music.
Psalm 57:7 (NIV)

One morning after my father's funeral, when I was back at home again, I found myself during my prayer time lost in sorrow, staring mutely at the wall. Reliving events of the preceding week and the many acts of kindness shown to our family, I suddenly wished for a way besides a card to express my gratitude to my parents' pastor and a few extraordinarily helpful neighbours.

I decided to make personalised, handmade gifts. While working on the gifts during the next several days, I found that instead of being lost in sorrow I was caught up in prayerful creativity. My mood improved dramatically, and by the time I took my offerings to the post office, I felt deeply comforted.

Now I recall this incident each time I read Psalm 57, written while its author was hiding in a cave, fearing for his life. David—the shepherd, the warrior, the king—was also a poet and a musician. Doubtless, his 'song in the dark' provided peace and reassurance to him, and now it does the same for us. It also reminds us that we all possess some creative ability, in music or handicrafts, in homemaking or business, that we can consecrate to God and use for the good of others. When we employ these skills—especially as we suffer through crisis and loss—we may find ourselves surprisingly encouraged.

Prayer: *Dear Lord, help us to use our talents to bless others, even when we are hurting. Amen*

Thought for the Day: Serving others brings light into dark days.

Link2Life: *List three of your talents and skills. Beside each one, list a way to use that skill for others.*

Deanna Overstreet (New Mexico)

Signposts

Read Romans 12:1–8

Jesus answered, 'I am the way and the truth and the life. No one comes to the Father except through me.'

John 14:6 (NIV)

On my way home from work recently, I delivered some books to a client. I thought I knew the way back to the main road and did not take any notice of the signs. Trusting my sense of direction resulted in a long detour and a lot of wasted time.

Later, reflecting on this incident, I realised that in many situations I trust my own sense of direction. I am ashamed that because I do not always depend on Jesus to show me the way, I stumble over obstacles. I do not look to God to show me the truth in all circumstances or to guide me in the perfect paths of life.

Since then, I have made a point of committing to the Lord each decision I make, asking God to show me the way I should go. By starting my day in prayer, studying and meditating on the word of God, and then quietly listening for God's guidance, I do not just act on impulse. Instead, acting at God's direction, I can experience the reassurance of knowing I am on the right road. When we follow what our Lord directs us to do, we can be assured of living a life of service, sustained by God's abundant grace.

Prayer: *Dear God, grant us grace to follow your directions and guidance. Through Jesus Christ our Lord. Amen*

Thought for the Day: Where do I find God's direction in my life?

Renny Stoltz (Gauteng, South Africa)

PRAYER FOCUS: THOSE WHO HAVE LOST THEIR WAY

A Prodigal's Return

Read Psalm 42:1–5

The father said to his servants, 'This son of mine was dead and is alive again; he was lost and is found.'
Luke 15:24 (NIV)

I had walked into a church hundreds of times before, but this time was different. I remember climbing up the steps, shaking hands with a couple of people, and then looking around to decide where I wanted to sit. It was all pretty normal. But then I started to cry. The same thing happened the next week, and the week after that.

I was surprised by my reaction because I do not cry often. What had happened? I'm quite sure it was because I had just rededicated my life to the Lord after many years of not taking my faith seriously.

Like many people, I had allowed my Christian faith to become a casual, rather insignificant part of my life. Yes, I believed in God, but I didn't think about God very much. I was living a busy life, and God was only one part of it—a very small part of it, unfortunately. My tears were about coming home to God, who accepted me despite my having largely ignored our relationship for a long time. The tears were about realising deep down that relationship with God is essential, a central part of who I am and who God created me to be.

Prayer: *Dear Father, thank you for welcoming us back when we return to you. Draw us close to you. Amen*

Thought for the Day: Relationship with God is the sure foundation for a good life.

James Davidson (Quebec, Canada)

More than Conquerors

Read Isaiah 40:28–31

We are more than conquerors through him who loved us.
Romans 8:37 (NRSV)

As a hospital chaplain, recently I went to visit a patient who had been ill for some time. When I entered the room, the patient said with a large sigh, 'The doctor was here just now and did not have very good news.'

I asked her what the doctor had said. In a sad and discouraged voice, she replied that the doctor said she would need to have extensive surgery. 'I know the Lord never gives you more than you can bear,' (see 1 Corinthians 10:13) she added, 'but I don't know where I will find the strength to get through this.'

I reminded her of the statement in Romans that we are more than conquerors through Christ and that regardless of what happens in our life, we are not limited to our own resources. If we turn our situation over to God and trust in Christ, we can rely on God's infinite strength and love to get us through.

After a moment she said, 'That is right. We don't have to do it ourselves, do we?' I then offered to pray with her for strength and trust.

Prayer: *Dear Lord, help us to turn our cares over to you and then to trust you to give us the strength to conquer fear. Amen*

Thought for the Day: No matter how fearsome our situation, Christ offers us strength.

Link2Life: *Volunteer to visit people in hospital.*

Timothy Hastings (Michigan)

Warts and All

Read 1 Chronicles 17:6–20

David prayed to the Lord, 'You know me well, and yet you honour me.'
1 Chronicles 17:18 (GNB)

When I was growing up, my parents set high standards for me. I met those standards more often than not, but I remember feeling that I got more attention when I didn't. For instance, they expected me to do well at school because they knew I could, and so I didn't get rewarded when I did well as some of my friends did. I did, however, get negative attention when my performance slipped.

Since we tend to view God through the lens of our experiences with our parents, I have had difficulty accepting the fact that God's love for me doesn't change based on my performance. God loves me just as much when I am failing as when I am succeeding. This kind of love doesn't make any sense to me; the only way I can even begin to believe in it is by reading about it over and over in the Bible.

David makes a good case study for this principle. He failed repeatedly, but God was still faithful to him. God promised that David's son would rule Israel. David knew he didn't deserve this from the minute he heard it; all he could do was pour out his thanks to God. I can't earn God's unfailing love either, but I can thank God for it and proclaim it daily.

Prayer: *O God, thank you for your unfailing love. Help me to trust in it and share it today. Amen*

Thought for the Day: God loves me, warts and all.

Link2Life: *Think about the ways in which God is like and not like your parents.*

Jennifer Aaron (Washington)

PRAYER FOCUS: YOUNG PEOPLE STRUGGLING AT SCHOOL

Hidden in the Mist

Read Exodus 24:12–18
While he was still speaking, a bright cloud enveloped them, and a voice from the cloud said, 'This is my Son.'
Matthew 17:5 (NIV)

The view from my study window is always an inspiration. Beyond the houses, across the fields and high up on a hill stands a church, its spire pointing to the sky. In the summer months the sun sets behind the church's silhouette, and the lengthening rays make it look like a picture postcard. On rare occasions the scene is highlighted with a covering of snow. Then it looks like a picture Christmas card.

It is not the church I attend, but I recognise it as a place of worship, a piece of ground where God is honoured and worshipped. Before I start writing each day, I look up to that church and pray for God's guidance. I use the view as a reminder of my purpose for writing. I feel that unless I dedicate my work to God, the result will be so much hay, straw and stubble, and in the end it will not endure.

Then one November day, I couldn't see the church. A thick mist veiled the view. I felt almost bereft, as if God had deserted me. How could I focus my prayer if I could not see the church?

Then I thought logically: the building was still there, even though I couldn't see it. People were still visiting it to pray and praise. In the same way God is still there, even when I cannot recognise him, or when my eyes are dim with grief or sadness. God has said he will never leave or forsake us. We may sometimes feel far from God, but he is never far from us.

Prayer: *O Lord, help us to remember that you are always with us, even when the world weighs heavy on us. Amen*

Thought for the Day: God is only a prayer away.

Carol Purves (Carlisle, England)

PRAYER FOCUS: THOSE WHO FIND IT HARD TO REACH GOD

I Will Care for You

Read Matthew 25:34–40

The king will answer [the righteous], 'Truly I tell you, just as you did it to one of the least of these who are members of my family, you did it to me.'
Matthew 25:40 (NRSV)

One morning as I was sharing the gospel with people in my village, an old woman came up to me. The day was bright, yet her face was gloomy and sad. I saw that she wanted to tell me something, but she uttered no word. I gave some rice to her, and her face brightened. She ate the rice as fast as she could.

'My son and his family have abandoned me,' she stammered. 'For two days I have had no food, and I was looking to you, Pastor. Please help me if you can. Otherwise…' She stopped as tears started flowing from her eyes.

I hugged her bony shoulders, telling her, 'Don't worry, Grandma, I will take you to my home and care for you.' In response, her eyes shone like stars in the night sky. My home became a refuge for this woman. After a year she died and went to be with the Lord.

Many in the world face overwhelming hopelessness. A little love, a touch, a smile and compassion from us can wipe away many tears. God can use us to turn sadness to happiness, to help another to live and to die with a sense of God's presence and love.

Prayer: *O Lord, give us eyes to see, hearts to love and hands to serve those in need. Amen*

Thought for the Day: Compassion is the blessed responsibility of God's people.

S. Rajan (Kerala, India)

Learning to Pray

Read Luke 11:1–13

Jesus said, 'Ask, and it will be given you; search, and you will find; knock, and the door will be opened for you.'

Luke 11:9 (NRSV)

I learned as a child to pray. My Sunday school teacher, Margarita, taught us to express gratitude to God. Like all children, we prayed for the flowers, the sky and little birds. Then Margarita became very ill, and Sunday school was no longer the same. We were all sad. Later I inquired about her and learned how truly ill she was. I remember thinking, at four years of age, that I needed to do something for her. That night I got down on my knees near my bed, and with all innocence and sincerity I asked Jesus in my short and simple prayer to heal Margarita.

After some time, Margarita was well, and I felt very happy because I had joined others in praying for her healing. My prayers were answered, as were my questions and doubts. I began a dialogue with God. This first intercessory prayer experience became the foundation of the discipline I follow to pray for others.

Prayer does not have to be difficult and there are no set formulas for the way we pray. We open our heart to God about concerns we have and joys we experience. If we need help with a decision, we ask and God will show us the way. When we need healing, God is at our side. And for the joys in our life, we express our gratitude.

Prayer: *We give thanks, loving God, that we are always united in the bond of prayer and sheltered in your grace. Amen*

Thought for the Day: Today I can begin a dialogue with God.

Link2Life: *Spend time with a child by reading the Bible and praying with them.*

Neri K. Gattinoni (Buenos Aires, Argentina)

True Golden Years

Read Jeremiah 17:5–8

My God will fully satisfy every need of yours according to his riches in glory in Christ Jesus. To our God and Father be glory forever and ever.
Philippians 4:19–20 (NRSV)

Since my recent retirement, my wife and I are learning more about budgeting, eating out less and limiting our spending. Perhaps the word that best describes retirement for us is 'overwhelming'.

Overwhelming, that is, if we leave God out of the picture. But we can be thankful that God remains constant. God's faithfulness to meet our needs is the same as it was before I retired. God is not limited to our limited resources. After all, God sustained thousands of Israelites with daily manna. And Jesus told Peter to extract money for taxes from the mouth of a fish (see Matthew 17:24–27). Jesus also took five loaves of bread and two small fish and fed over 5,000 people.

Drawing on the images in today's Bible reading, when we have the option of being a brown bush in the dry wasteland or a green tree planted by the water, our choice is obvious. I particularly like the part in the reading about having 'no worries' (Jeremiah 17:8, NIV). Because of God's faithfulness, my retirement is blessed, not cursed; fruitful, not barren; prosperous, not wanting. God's faithfulness changes 'overwhelming' to 'overcoming'.

Prayer: *Thank you, Lord, for your faithfulness to us in all the circumstances of our lives. Amen*

Thought for the Day: Life is not about what we earn; it's about what God provides.

Thomas Buice (Florida)

The Gift of Faith

Read Matthew 11:25–28

Jesus said, 'What I say to you in the dark, tell in the light; and what you hear whispered, proclaim from the housetops.'
Matthew 10:27 (NRSV)

I grew up an atheist, receiving an atheist education at home, school and college. I earned a degree in natural sciences (medicine and biology) and was firmly convinced that God was an invention of uneducated people. In the hospital where I worked, Christians were among my colleagues; but they hid the fact that they believed in God. The only person with whom I talked about religion was a nurse. However, I did not conduct atheist conversations with her. She gave me my first lessons in the Christian faith. Because of our talks, for the first time, I started thinking about the possibility that we atheists were wrong.

At the age of 60, thanks to my acquaintance, I accepted Christ into my heart, was baptised and became a Christian. I suddenly discovered a whole world that had previously been unknown to me.

When I moved to a new village, I felt lonely. God led me to a new church. I made new Christian friends and was no longer lonely. After a while, I began to lead a Bible class in which I told church members about the gospel and about Jesus. Now I wonder, 'How was it possible for me to live without God before?'

Prayer: *Dear God, thank you for saving faith in Jesus Christ, our Saviour, and for the joy of being a Christian. Amen.*

Thought for the Day: Believing in Christ opens the door to a whole new world.

Galina Vyugova (Krasnodar, Russia)

Hope in All Situations

Read Romans 8:35–39

Jesus said, 'I tell you the truth: It is for your good that I am going away. Unless I go away, the Counsellor will not come to you; but if I go, I will send him to you.'
John 16:7 (NIV)

'I don't want to die, but I'm not afraid to die,' my dad told the nurse. Dad's condition was so serious that he was not expected to leave the hospital. In the discussion that followed, we talked with the nurse about how Stephen had looked into the heavens and seen Christ's face as he was being stoned. Also, we quoted Paul when he said, 'To live is Christ and to die is gain' (Philippians 1:21, NIV).

My dad was not afraid to die because his eyes were set on his heavenly home. In heaven he would face no more sickness, worries or tears. All of his earthly troubles would be gone.

All Christians have the assurance that God will be with us whatever the trial or hardship, even when we face death. Jesus knew that after his crucifixion his disciples would feel lost and abandoned, so he sent the Holy Spirit to comfort them. We can have that same comfort as 'we fix our eyes not on what is seen, but on what is unseen. For what is seen is temporary, but what is unseen is eternal' (2 Corinthians 4:18, NIV).

Prayer: *Dear Lord, help us to keep our eyes on you through all our trials and hardships. Amen*

Thought for the Day: God is with us in all our struggles and transitions.

Wayne Gemeinhardt (Alabama)

PRAYER FOCUS: THOSE NEAR DEATH

Trusting God

Read Matthew 6:25–34

Strive first for the kingdom of God and his righteousness, and all these things will be given to you as well.
Matthew 6:33 (NRSV)

Yesterday I rose early and caught the morning ferry across the river. The day was clear and sunny, and I was enjoying the view across the water. The ferry was not crowded, and the trip was peaceful.

I quietly began to pray, giving thanks to God for the many blessings in my life: my wife, my family, my job and a baby on the way. Before long, my thoughts turned anxious: 'What if the economy continues to worsen, and I lose my job? What if the baby isn't healthy? What if? What if?' Instead of praising God, I began seeking God's assurance, asking for security.

At that moment, the ferry began to slow; and the captain's voice came over the loudspeaker. He announced that thick fog was ahead but that we would still reach our destination on time. Peering ahead, I saw the shoreline disappear behind a heavy curtain of white. I thought of the crew trusting the boat's instruments to navigate.

In Matthew 6:25–34, Jesus encourages us to trust the navigation of our lives to God. While we can see the present and past, the future is unclear and foggy. Not knowing what's ahead can be a source of great anxiety. But Christ assures us that we can find peace in trusting God and in being open to God's will. I closed my prayer with praise.

Prayer: *God of all times and places, teach us to rely on you for all we need. Amen*

Thought for the Day: Give your anxieties to God.

Erik Tingelstad (Washington)

The Runaway

Read Luke 15:11–24

Where can I flee from your presence? … If I take the wings of the morning and settle at the farthest limits of the sea, even there your hand shall lead me, and your right hand shall hold me fast.
Psalm 139:7, 9, 10 (NRSV)

Years ago when I was a child, I lay in a nest of tall weeds under an apple tree and came to the conclusion that my life as a seven-year-old was too hard. Running away was the solution. A life of living on the soft grass, eating apples in the warm sunshine, was inviting. When I informed my mother of my decision, she covered her dismay by advising me to take some clean underwear with me.

I immediately put my plan into action and basked in my new-found freedom, munching on an apple. Several apples later, as the chill of evening began to invade my nest, the thought of my warm home only a few streets away began to disturb my peace.

I trudged home in the fading light, entering the brightly lit house just as my family was settling down to dinner. My place had been set, and my mother showed no surprise at my appearance. She expected me. Even though I had tried to run away from her discipline and care, her caring did not leave me. She had let me know that I would always be her son. And being her son, I was allowed to live in the warm house with love, security and hearty food instead of in the cold weeds, with apples, alone in the dark of night.

We can never outrun God, who has promised never to leave us or forsake us. Like the prodigal, when we come home we will always be welcome.

Prayer: *Thank you for always being there, Lord, so that we don't have to face life alone. Amen*

Thought for the Day: We have a home with the Lord at any time.
Fred W. Buehling (Oregon)

PRAYER FOCUS: PARENTS OF MISSING CHILDREN

Be Bold!

Read Matthew 15:21–28

Let us… approach the throne of grace with confidence, so that we may receive mercy and find grace to help us in our time of need.
Hebrews 4:16 (NIV)

My baby's shrill shriek sent me running to the nursery. When I got there, I discovered that he had apparently stopped breathing. Panicked, my husband and I rushed to the hospital, bearing what looked like a dead child. Anxious and afraid, I prayed aloud, as if hearing my spoken plea would boost my faith. The hospital staff looked at me as if I were crazy. Still I prayed persistently, begging God to save my baby. I was desperate, and didn't care what people thought. When the doctor announced that against all odds our baby was all right, I thanked God.

The Canaanite mother in Matthew 15 also sought Jesus to heal her child. But Jesus' response to her pleas was startling. He first ignored and then rebuffed her, seeming to echo the disciples' annoyance. But the desperate mother didn't care how others perceived her. She didn't give up asking Jesus to heal her child. She persisted, and her child was healed.

God is sovereign and knows more about this world and its workings than we do. And God doesn't always heal when we pray for healing. However, we can still go to God boldly with our needs. And God always listens. Our faith always pleases God—no matter what other people may think and no matter what the outcome.

Prayer: *Dear Lord Jesus, please help us to be bold about voicing our requests and not intimidated by what anyone may think. Amen*

Thought for the Day: Pray boldly and trust God.

Janey L. DeMeo (California)

Fragrance for the World

Read James 1:19–27

Paul wrote, 'Do not be deceived: "Bad company ruins good morals."'
1 Corinthians 15:33 (NRSV)

Packing hurriedly after a long church conference, I shoved my dirty laundry into my suitcase along with my clean clothes. I thought that when I got home I could wash the dirty clothes and wear the clean clothes. But when I opened my suitcase to unpack, the acrid smell of old sweat rolled out. The odour of my dirty clothes had permeated my clean clothes.

Something similar can happen in our social interactions as well. Sometimes young people at church ask me if it's OK to have friends who are not Christians. 'Absolutely,' I tell them. 'In fact, I think you should. But always ask yourself, "Am I rubbing off on them, or are they rubbing off on me?"' Peer pressure can be just as great for adults. Negativity, gossip, prejudice and greed can all be contagious. But so can love, joy, peace, patience, kindness, generosity, faithfulness, gentleness and self-control (Galatians 5:22–23, NRSV).

Today's reading from James cautions us to keep ourselves 'unstained by the world' (James 1:27, NRSV). Certainly this does not invite us to be aloof or self-righteous. But this admonition does remind us that we must not allow ourselves to be overpowered by worldly society. Instead, we should be the stronger influence, spreading the love of Christ by our example (see 2 Corinthians 2: 14–16).

Prayer: *Dear Lord, help us to allow Christ to be the greatest influence on our lives, so that his light may shine through us. Amen*

Thought for the Day: God calls us to have a positive impact on our environment.

Michael Raypholtz (Ohio)

Not Alone!*

Read Psalm 91

I will lead the blind by a road they do not know, by paths they have not known I will guide them. I will turn the darkness before them into light, the rough places into level ground. These are the things I will do, and I will not forsake them.
Isaiah 42:16 (NRSV)

I was in South Korea on a work assignment. I could not read, speak or understand the Korean language; and most Koreans I met could not understand my English dialect. I was facing a serious communication challenge. Because I was working in the telecommunications industry, this seemed to be an irony—especially since I needed to travel by train 200 kilometres to the capital city of Seoul on my own. I was very anxious.

God responded to my silent prayer; I sensed an assurance that I was not alone. Help soon came in the form of a smiling young man who somehow grasped my predicament. With an impromptu type of sign language, he helped me purchase the necessary train ticket and alerted me when I needed to get off the train some hours later. I will always remember his smiling face and his amazing ability to sense my need.

When has God sent an angel to direct, comfort or encourage you?

Prayer: *God of all the world, thank you for your love and your guidance, no matter where in this world we may be. Amen*

Thought for the Day: Look for God in those around you, wherever you are.

* To celebrate our 75th Anniversary, we have included this meditation which was originally published on 19 April 2008.

Roland Rink (Gauteng, South Africa)

Don't Look Back!

Read Philippians 3:10–17

Paul wrote, 'One thing I do: Forgetting what is behind and straining toward what is ahead, I press on toward the goal to win the prize for which God has called me heavenward in Christ Jesus.'

Philippians 3:13–14 (NIV)

Several years ago, I had the chance to go on a boat trip with my brother-in-law, Ben, and some members of his family. I sat behind Ben, who was also steering the boat.

At times during the trip, Ben blocked my view; I was not able to see all the beauty of the water, sky and trees ahead—the view I loved the most. But looking back for a different view didn't help because when I looked back, I would begin to feel sick. Eventually, I learned my lesson: don't look back! Only when I kept my eyes focused forward was I able to enjoy the boat trip without nausea.

When life is hard or seems to be changing too fast for us, it's easy to look back and long for the 'good old days', when life seemed better. But, while treasuring fond memories of the past isn't wrong, the Bible makes it clear that we can forget the past and go forward with Christ. With his help, we can make each of our days a gift to God.

Prayer: *Dear loving God, no matter how we view our past, give us the grace and strength we need to leave it behind and go forward with you. In Jesus' name. Amen*

Thought for the Day: We can't look to the future while looking at the past.

Link2Life: *Make a list of your regrets, then burn it and give thanks to God for the chance to begin again.*

Tyler Myers (Ohio)

PRAYER FOCUS: THOSE STRUGGLING TO LEAVE THE PAST BEHIND

Everything Belongs to God

Read Genesis 2:4–15

The earth is the Lord's and all that is in it, the world, and those who live in it.

Psalm 24:1 (NRSV)

I live in a country where the standard of living is high. But our lifestyle has far-reaching effects. If everyone used as many of Earth's resources per person as we do in Denmark, we would need about two extra planets the size of this one to sustain the world's population.

God created the world and saw that it was good. God gave humans the responsibility of being stewards of creation. But we use nature as if it were an infinite resource. We treat creation as if we own it and can use it as we please.

We do not own Earth. God does. As children are a gift and a responsibility for their parents, Earth, God's gift to us, comes with responsibility for its care. God's creation sustains our existence, providing land, water and the air that keeps us alive.

When I make decisions about my lifestyle—choices about food, clothing, transportation—I try to remember that the earth belongs to God. I am part of God's creation, and God's creation keeps me alive. Creation is God's way of taking care of us.

Prayer: *Thank you, God, for creating the world and all that is in it: friends, family, fish, spiders, swallows, wheat, water and oxygen. Forgive us when we abuse your good gifts. Help us to make responsible choices that help other people and honour your creation. Amen*

Thought for the Day: The world and all that is in it belong to God—not to me.

Hanna Smidt (Hovedstaden, Denmark)

Beautiful Moments

Read Luke 10:38–42

She had a sister named Mary, who sat at the Lord's feet and listened to what he was saying.
Luke 10:39 (NRSV)

In the middle of morning service at our church, four-year-old Lydia ran up the aisle and sat down at her father's feet as he was about to lead us in prayer. He reached down and stroked her hair as he continued. All through the prayers Lydia remained perfectly still and quiet, playing with her fingers and occasionally looking up at him. It was a beautiful moment!

Watching that child reminded me of the incident in Luke's Gospel when Mary sat attentively at Jesus' feet, in contrast to her over-busy and resentful sister, Martha. Mary, we can be sure, wasn't often sitting doing nothing, and had no doubt been just as busy as Martha with preparations before their guest arrived. But for the duration of his visit she made the most of the opportunity to give Jesus her undivided attention. When Martha objected, Jesus gently pointed out to her the value of Mary's action.

How often, like Martha, do we miss or waste opportunities to be still and draw new strength and peace from listening to the Lord? Many necessary things demand our time and attention but there comes a point when we need the wisdom to leave them, even if they are unfinished, and make Jesus our priority.

Prayer: *Lord Jesus, please help us to know when to put our busy activities on one side and fix our attention on you. Amen*

Thought for the Day: Make time to stop, be still and recognise the Lord's presence.

Hazel V. Thompson (Somerset, England)

PRAYER FOCUS: PEOPLE STRUGGLING WITH HEAVY RESPONSIBILITIES

The Death of Civility

'What is the most important thing in the world to you?' My friend's wife was confronting him about working excessive hours, trying to help him see what he was doing to their family by his absence. He said, 'I had to think long and hard before I answered. Finally, I said, "Relationships. Relationships are the most important thing."'

He was right. God wants for us loving relationships where people are respected and honoured as the unique and dearly loved children of God that they are, that each one of us is. But more and more our interactions, even interactions among Christians, are characterised by harsh and polarising language. In radio and television programmes and in conversations at church, we hear Christians berating and belittling others. Shouldn't we model a better way? Can we, as Ephesians 4:15 says, speak 'the truth in love'?

Differences are inevitable. Unity in Christ does not mean uniformity; it never has. In the first years of the Christian movement, differences about keeping holidays divided the believers in Rome. They also argued whether or not it was permissible for Christians to eat meat that had been offered to idols. (Once the sacrificed animal died, it was butchered and the meat sold in the public market.) Paul cautioned the believers against 'quarrelling over opinions' (Romans 14:1, NRSV). Paul went on to tell them not to judge one another, for, 'Who are you to pass judgment on servants of another? It is before their own lord that they stand or fall' (Romans 14:4, NRSV).

Since the first century, faithful, reasonable and well-meaning Christians have differed on other serious issues. For example, for the first few centuries of the church, Christians refused to bear arms. Many Christians (some denominations) remain pacifist today, while other equally faithful and committed believers subscribe to the theory of 'just' war. In the 1800s, denominations split over the question of whether Christians could own slaves. Abolitionists worked to end slavery because of what the Bible teaches, and slaveholders quoted the Bible to support their position. You can probably list many other differences of opinion and interpretations of 'what the Bible says'. But our differences in politics, gender, race and age are far less important than the fact that we all are children of God.

What is troubling about our having differences is the strident tone of our public and private discussions of them. These include denunciations and even questioning one another's Christian commitment. The Bible tells us to avoid 'arguments and quarrels' because they are 'unprofitable and useless' (Titus 3:9, NIV) and to respond to one another 'with gentleness and respect' (1 Peter 3:15, NIV). No matter what our views are, we are called to deal gently and lovingly with each other, without judging or badgering one another. We are not to call another person names. Reducing others to a label keeps us from truly knowing and learning from them.

Trying to argue others into changing their opinions is futile. If we cannot convince ourselves to do good things like eating more wisely or saving more, how can we hope to change someone else's mind? This is not to say that we should not speak the truth as we understand it. But we do so always with humility, honestly admitting that as sure as we may be of our stance, there is a possibility that we are wrong.

We are not in charge of what others believe, and we can trust God's ongoing work in each of us (Philippians 1:6). When we treat others with love and respect, we participate in God's loving work of forming each of us more fully into the image of Christ. Then these others travel on, as we do, along the path God sets uniquely before each of us.

As my friend said, relationships are the most important thing. Deciding to love others by listening to them and speaking lovingly to them is a spiritual discipline. When we choose to love in the way we speak to one another, we show that God lives in us. Paul prayed for the Roman Christians to live in love so they might 'with one voice glorify... God' (Romans 15:6, NRSV). We begin by loving those close to us, moving ever outward to love the world as God loves it. People said of the first Christians, 'Behold how they love one another!' May those who hear our words and witness our interactions be able to say the same of us.

You may want to re-read the meditations for 8, 9, 11, 13, 16, 23 and 25 September, 1, 5, 6 and 10 October, 23 November, and 16 and 31 December as you consider the reflection questions below.

Questions for Reflection:

1. What kinds of discussions challenge you to listen and speak lovingly? How might you behave differently if you were to picture Christ as the person before you, speaking the words you are hearing?

2. Do you believe that Christians should work toward agreeing on political and social issues? If so, why and how? If not, why not?

3. If a non-Christian were to overhear your last comments about someone with whom you disagree on something important, what conclusions might they draw about Christians' attitudes? Would you want them to repeat what they heard?

4. Jesus taught us to love our enemies. Who are yours? How might you love them more faithfully? How can you show love in the way you speak to and about them?

5. What subjects and people did you think of as you read these pages? What is God nudging you to say or do in regard to them?

6. With what parts of this article do you agree or disagree? Why? How might you express these disagreements in a loving way?

Mary Lou Redding

Not Just Another Book*

Read Acts 8:26–40

More to be desired are [the ordinances of the Lord] than gold, even much fine gold; sweeter also than honey, and drippings of the honeycomb.
Psalm 19:10 (NRSV)

Copies of the New Testament were being handed out by our religious studies teacher. They were regarded by some of my school friends as just another book on which they needed to put a protective cover—one more to cram into an already-overflowing, messy desk. Here was something else to add to the load of a heavy school bag.

For those of us who knew and loved the New Testament, the book meant something more. We were quite happy to cover the books on the outside, but how much more we wanted to open them and point out the 'good news' to those friends for whom what is inside was covered up, too. How we wanted to tell them that the Bible is not just another book to cover! It is a gift to show the world.

Prayer: *Help us, Lord, to take our Bibles out of their covers and share the good news with everyone we know. Amen*

Thought for the Day: When have I shared the good news of the Bible?

* To celebrate our 75th Anniversary, we have included this meditation which was originally published on 1 November 1987. When she wrote this meditation, Nicola Priest Vidamour was a 14-year-old student. Today, after living for six years in Russia, she is the editor of *Mesto Vstrechi* (the Russian edition of *The Upper Room*). The first meditation that *Mesto Vstrechi* published appeared on 1 November 2008—exactly 21 years after Nicola's first meditation was published in *The Upper Room*. Her latest meditation appears on 6 December.

Nicola Priest (England)

At the Border

Read 1 Corinthians 13:8–13

Love never ends.
1 Corinthians 13:8 (NRSV)

Last Monday the 31-year-old son of a church colleague died at the end of a six-month battle with cancer. He and his wife have a two-month-old son. What can I say as a pastor at times like this? What could any of us say? Theologian and father Karl Barth offers some help. Standing at the grave of his 20-year-old son, Barth seized on the apostle Paul's words 'now' and 'then' in 1 Corinthians 13. These two words define the boundary between this life and the life to come.

We stood at that painful border on Monday morning. The doctors had done their best; cancer had done its worst. There are so many questions we want to ask, don't know how to ask or are afraid to ask. Paul acknowledges that in this life we don't have all the answers.

Our hope is in the promise of 'then'. On the other side of resurrection, we will see God face to face. 'Then' we will understand fully, even as we have been fully understood by God. Now we see dimly; then we will see face to face. Now we know in part; then we will know fully. In times of grief, three essential qualities link our 'now' with God's 'then': faith, hope and love. And the greatest—the gift that crosses the boundary between this life and the life to come—is love. May God's love be made real in us for those around us 'now', as a taste of 'then'.

Prayer: *O God, help us entrust all our unanswered and unanswerable questions to your amazing love. Amen*

Thought for the Day: Love is stronger than death.

James A. Harnish (Florida)

PRAYER FOCUS: PARENTS WHOSE CHILD HAS DIED RECENTLY

Buy Less, Give More

Read Luke 12:22–34
Where your treasure is, there your heart will be also.
Luke 12:34 (NIV)

One afternoon, my husband and I went for a three-hour drive to pick up some machinery to use in our wheat harvest. The first part of the trip was along a road I had travelled many times; the last was in new territory. On the new road I was excited to see a sign for a market. 'Oh! That looks like fun!' I said. But then I realised we really didn't need to buy anything.

I have come to see that the less I buy, the more money I have to give to charity, to church and to other ministries. I'm learning to live more simply because I'm thankful for what God has done in my life. Out of that gratitude I want to give and to help others come to know and worship God also.

I certainly haven't mastered the art of frugal living. I love books and magazines far too much. And I'm not as careful with our household budget as I could be. But I've found that not only does buying less allow me to give more money away; owning less that I have to care for gives me more time to spend with God and to serve others.

Prayer: *Thank you, God, that you are our great provider. Help us to be content with what we have so that we can give more. Amen*

Thought for the Day: If we live more simply, we can give more generously.

Link2Life: *Have a look at the clothes in your wardrobe. How many of these do you have? How many do you actually need?*

Rebecca Stuhlmiller (Washington)

Directions

Read Psalm 25:1–10
Stand at the crossroads, and look, and ask for the ancient paths, where the good way lies; and walk in it, and find rest for your souls.
Jeremiah 6:16 (NRSV)

A distressed driver stopped me as I walked, and announced that she was completely lost. Agitated and berating our town's apparent lack of signposts, she told me she was late for an appointment. I knew exactly where she wanted to go and how to get there. I explained the correct way slowly and clearly, despite her impatience. 'If you listen,' I found myself saying, 'you won't get lost.' She nodded, relaxed, then reversed her car and disappeared from view.

As I watched her go, I wondered how often I ask God for direction but don't stop and listen. Am I just speeding on in life or rushing through the day with just a cursory glance heavenward? This stranger was a timely reminder to me of my need to study God's word, the Bible, more closely and to take the time to listen receptively to God.

Prayer: *Thank you, heavenly Father, that you always have your eye upon us, that you always desire to lead us, and that you always want to make your ways known to us. As Jesus taught us, we pray, 'Our Father which art in heaven, Hallowed be thy name. Thy kingdom come. Thy will be done, as in heaven, so in earth. Give us day by day our daily bread. And forgive us our sins; for we also forgive every one that is indebted to us. And lead us not into temptation; but deliver us from evil.'* Amen*

Thought for the Day: If we listen to the Spirit and obey God's word, we can find our way.

Link2Life: *Are the signs in your church clear and helpful?*

Hilary Allen (Somerset, England)

PRAYER FOCUS: THOSE LIVING IN STRESSFUL SITUATIONS
* Luke 11:2–4 (KJV)

No Longer Strangers*

Read Ephesians 2:11–22
You shall also love the stranger, for you were strangers in the land of Egypt.
Deuteronomy 10:19 (NRSV)

Sunday morning worship was over, and I was waiting to enter the aisle that led to the door. A man I had never seen before made his way to the end of another pew, placed a bulky rucksack near the crowded centre aisle, then reversed direction and moved away. I felt a surge of alarm. Not every rucksack-bearing stranger is a potential threat, of course, but indiscriminate acts of terrorism have given rise to indiscriminate suspicion as well.

Before I could react, a member of our congregation approached the newcomer, offering his hand in welcome. Genuine pleasure illuminated the man's face and, as the two chatted at length, my anxiety abated.

My neighbour's response not only affirmed for me the reality that Jesus has removed obstacles separating people from God and each other but demonstrated the healing potential of Christian hospitality as well. Such hospitality blesses all those it touches: those who extend it, those who accept it, and those who, like me, witness it!

Prayer: *Loving God, teach us to walk in wisdom, courage and love. Help us show the hospitality that welcomes others into your presence. Amen*

Thought for the Day: Christian hospitality can break down walls of fear and suspicion.

* To celebrate our 75th Anniversary, we have included this meditation which was originally published on 17 December 2000.

William T. Haes (New Jersey)

The Right Moves

Read John 14:11–18

I am the Lord, your God, who takes hold of your right hand and says to you, Do not fear; I will help you.
Isaiah 41:13 (NIV)

I like to play some very challenging games on my computer. Many of them give me hints about making my next move, guiding me to more advanced levels of play. Often, however, I allow my independent spirit to take over, and I ignore these hints, trying to master the game with my own moves. As a consequence, my progress is much slower—or I fail completely and have to start again. But when I take advantage of the built-in help features, I improve my skills and move on to more difficult challenges.

In a much more important way, in our spiritual life we are also meant to move to new levels. After his death, Jesus told his disciples that they would move on to incredible levels of responsibility. However, Jesus also assured them that if they asked, the Holy Spirit would help and guide them. When I am faced with obstacles in my daily Christian living, God also offers me the Holy Spirit to guide my moves.

By studying God's word, praying daily and listening to the still, small voice (1 Kings 19:12, KJV) of the Spirit in my mind, heart and will, I access the 'help features' that God provides for us. When I choose to ask for help and obey God's commands, God will show me how to move to the next level of my Christian discipleship.

Prayer: *Loving Father, help us always to rely on you to show us the next step as we live to follow your will. Amen*

Thought for the Day: God waits for us to ask for help—and then gives it.

Joni Melnick (Pennsylvania)

Open Doors

Read Romans 10:12–18

Always be prepared to give an answer to everyone who asks you to give the reason for the hope that you have. But do this with gentleness and respect.

1 Peter 3:15 (NIV)

One day I came to the checkout humming a gospel tune. The assistant said, 'You certainly seem happy today.' Bingo! A door opened. I replied, 'Every day is a great day when you have Jesus in your heart.' This opened the door for me to speak another word about my faith the next time I saw her.

God is always working, and every day offers opportunities to proclaim the good news. Whether we are at the supermarket, the petrol station, the shopping centre or on the street, opportunities arise. Paul says in Colossians 4:3 (NIV), 'Pray for us, too, that God may open a door for our message, so that we may proclaim the mystery of Christ.' Every day before leaving the house, I pray, 'Lord, help me to see the open doors today, and give me the courage to tell someone the good news of Jesus Christ.'

Doors of opportunity open for every believer, and many people need to hear of God's grace. Who is willing to talk about the wonderful grace of Jesus Christ? If you and I don't tell them, who will?

Prayer: *Dear God, open doors of opportunity so that we may tell the good news of Christ each day. Amen*

Thought for the Day: Doors of opportunity open for those who are willing to step through them.

Link2Life: *Prepare a list of what God has done for you so you are ready to speak when chances come, or look for ways to speak of your faith to those around you.*

Robert Delaney (Missouri)

PRAYER FOCUS: FOR COURAGE TO SPEAK ABOUT MY FAITH

Thoughts that Build

Read 2 Corinthians 4:8–12

What [the Lord] opens no one can shut, and what he shuts no one can open.
Revelation 3:7 (NIV)

The subject line of the e-mail message was 'Regret Letter'. Even before I opened the e-mail, I knew my job interview had been unsuccessful. My spirit was crushed, more so because this was the first interview I had had in a long time, and I had done my best to prepare for it. I felt professionally irrelevant and thought no one would be interested in offering me a job. While I was reading my Bible a week later, however, a verse in Jude leaped out at me: 'But you, dear friends, build yourselves up in your most holy faith and pray in the Holy Spirit (v. 20, NIV).

The verse's context was not related to my current circumstance, but these words helped me to see that I had been tearing myself down with negative thoughts and feelings. Praying in the Holy Spirit took my eyes off the closed door and moved my focus onto the Lord. My spirit was revived, and I knew all I had to do was trust that God would open the perfect opportunity, at the perfect time.

Prayer: *Dear Lord, thank you for the peace and assurance that comes from knowing that our future is secure in your hands, even when we cannot see an open door. Amen*

Thought for the Day: Focusing on the Lord builds us up; focusing only on our circumstances can tear us down.

Colleta N. Macharia (Lusaka, Zambia)

The Lead Role?

Read 2 Kings 5:1–14

The servant girl said to Naaman's wife, 'If only my master would see the prophet who is in Samaria! He would cure him of his leprosy.'
2 Kings 5:3 (NIV)

If this story were being made into a Hollywood movie, the title role of Naaman would probably be played by a famous, handsome leading man. On the other hand, the part of the nameless captive girl would probably be played by a less-than-famous, less-than-glamorous character actress. But in fact the girl captive is central to the plot. God chooses to heal Naaman through Elisha not because Naaman had won any particular favour from God: Naaman's healing was to demonstrate to the unnamed, doubting king of Israel that 'there is a prophet in Israel', that God was active in that time and place. In this story, the lives of both the captive girl and Naaman reveal God's power.

We are often told that the world does not revolve around us. But the story of Naaman and the captive girl suggests that even our own lives do not revolve around us. We are not stars of our own biographical movies but players in the larger story of God's kingdom. 'What have I done to deserve this?' is not the right question in times of either blessing or tribulation. Instead we can ask, 'How can I be useful in God's kingdom in my present circumstances?'

Prayer: *O God, help us to see our role in your story and to live it faithfully. Amen*

Thought for the Day: Each one of us has a role to play in God's story of redeeming the world.

Michael Macdonald (North Carolina)

A Worn Bible

Read 2 Timothy 3:14–17
The word of God is living and active.
Hebrews 4:12 (NIV)

Today it happened: I finally have a Bible like Gail's. Gail was one of the best Sunday school teachers I've ever had. She had a way of weaving together everyday life and the Bible. I wanted a Bible like Gail's. Obviously, she had the best reference Bible available. Her vast knowledge of the Bible poured out of her as she taught.

As she started class each Sunday morning, she would clutch her Bible in her right hand. Once, a page fluttered this way and others floated that way. The cover was worn off. Gail's Bible was falling apart from use. Gail could teach our class as she did not because she had a particular study Bible but because she studied the Bible she had.

Hebrews 4:12 tells us that God's word is full of living power. We can experience this spiritual power as we read the Bible and let its message sink into our soul. Then when trouble comes and we search for answers, the Bible will lead us to life-giving insights. The more we read our Bibles, the more wear and tear they show.

So today it happened. After 30 years of use, the cover of my Bible fell off. Finally I have a Bible like Gail's.

Prayer: *Dear God, lead us to read the Bible today and every day. Amen*

Thought for the Day: As our Bibles fall apart from use, we grow stronger.

Donna Riner Weber (Tennessee)

Keeping the Prize in Mind

Read Hebrews 12:1–3

I press on toward the goal for the prize of the heavenly call of God in Christ Jesus.
Philippians 3:14 (NRSV)

After watching the news of the death of the world's fattest man, I resolved to get in shape. To strengthen my body, I started taking a brisk walk each evening. As I began my walk, I was full of zeal; but after three laps of the neighbourhood park, I grew a little tired. I decided I needed an incentive to keep me going. Thinking of a reward I would receive at the end of my walk motivated me to complete my planned walk and kept my mind off my tiredness. One night the prize was sushi at a Japanese restaurant. Whenever I wanted to stop, I would say 'sushi', and that was enough to keep me going. Another evening, I thought of my plan to watch a movie. The key word I repeated to myself was 'movie'. Each evening thinking of a new reward spurred me on.

Sometimes we grow tired in our spiritual journey. Paul said, 'I press on toward the goal for the prize of the heavenly call of God in Christ Jesus.' When we tire in our spiritual journey, we can remember that the greatest motivation we have as Christians is seeing Christ face-to-face at the finishing line and sharing in his eternal glory.

Prayer: *Heavenly Lord, help us to keep the prize in mind so that we will keep going and growing in faith. Amen*

Thought for the Day: What can I do to keep my eyes on what God wants for me?

Mary Ng Shwu Ling (Singapore)

PRAYER FOCUS: THOSE STRUGGLING IN THEIR SPIRITUAL JOURNEY

Not Alone!

Read John 4:46–53

Jesus said to [the official], 'Go; your son will live.'
John 4:50 (NRSV)

My beautiful, athletic wife sat on the edge of the stretcher, squeezing my hand and staring intently ahead. Garbled words poured from her mouth as she struggled to speak. Frantically, Pat looked at me through tear-filled eyes. The paramedics had rushed her to the hospital from a cheerful outing with friends. The initial diagnosis had been a stroke, but now X-rays were showing tumours in her chest and head; the revised probability was cancer. Pat was admitted to the hospital for extensive examination and testing.

Over the next few days, many people began praying daily for Pat. The loving concern of Christian friends buoyed us and brought her a measure of peace. People rallied round, offering prayers, hope and practical help as we received confirmation of cancer in various parts of her body. Aggressive treatment began immediately.

There are times now when we feel like tightrope walkers, inching along a wire, high over a chasm in a strong wind. But then we think of our 'safety net'—our fellow Christians and the steady outpouring of heartfelt messages of prayer that reinforce our confidence, courage and hope. The journey would be almost impossible without this support. We take joy and strength from the certainty that we are not alone and that we are in God's hands. Praise God!

Prayer: *God of compassion, into your hands we place our loved ones and ourselves. In Jesus' name we pray. Amen*

Thought for the Day: Our prayers make a difference.

Link2Life: *This week, pray daily for the people listed on your church's prayer list.*

E.H. Eudy (Florida)

PRAYER FOCUS: THOSE BEING TREATED FOR CANCER

The Light of God

Read Isaiah 60:1–2, 18–22
I, the Lord, will be your eternal light, more lasting than the sun and moon.
Isaiah 60:20 (GNB)

The lighting of the lamp at nightfall took on a deeply ceremonial nature in my grandmother's house. Cleaned and filled with oil, the lamp was set on the table. The mantle of the lamp, the element that glows, was heated with a methylated spirit flame. Then came the great moment when the plunger built up pressure and the lamp suddenly burst into brilliant light, illuminating the centre of the room, heralding the arrival of supper, and bringing comfort and relaxation after the work and toil of the day.

The sense of comfort symbolised by that lamp and the dramatic change from darkness to light are surely what Isaiah meant when he talked about the people of Israel having the light of God shining upon them. In his vision of the glorious future with God, the change is so complete that violence and destruction will be no more; grief will come to an end. There will be no darkness, and that light is not dependent on being rekindled again and again.

The light of God shines upon us too, and in that light we find life and comfort and guidance along our way.

Prayer: *Loving Father, you have kindled a light that cannot be put out. In times of difficulty and grief and hopelessness, let your glorious light shine in our hearts to strengthen and comfort us. Amen*

Thought for the Day: The light of God shining upon us is like no other light; it cannot be extinguished.

W.M.M. Campbell (Aberdeen, Scotland)

PRAYER FOCUS: THOSE WHO NEED GOD'S LIGHT

The Music of Praise

Read Psalm 100

Then Miriam the prophetess, Aaron's sister, took a tambourine in her hand, and all the women followed her, with tambourines and dancing. Miriam sang to them: 'Sing to the Lord, for he is highly exalted.'
Exodus 15:20–21 (NIV)

My church regularly requests more Sunday school teachers, volunteers to pray aloud or people to work in finance, preaching and counselling. Although I haven't volunteered for one of these jobs, that doesn't mean I don't participate in the life of my church.

Like Miriam from the Exodus story, I have been blessed with musical talent that my parents cultivated when I was growing up. I sing in the choir, play handbells and play my flute in worship when I am asked. On occasion, our church music director has even handed me a tambourine to play along with one group or another. I have a reputation within the church for being reliable and helpful, but I'm really just using the talent God gave me to help the church in the best way I know.

I praise God with my music, while others praise by teaching, praying or counting the offering. We can each praise God—with whatever gifts and talents God has given us.

Prayer: *Lord God, we want to praise you the best way we know. We pray that through our gifts you will be glorified. Amen*

Thought for the Day: The best way to thank God for a gift is to give it back.

Kim Sheard (Virginia)

God's Masterpiece

Read Matthew 11:28–30

Can any of you by worrying add a single hour to your span of life?
Matthew 6:27 (NRSV)

One November night, Ottawa received its first substantial snowfall of the season. The next morning, instead of catching my bus to work, I first cleared the driveway for my wife. This decision interrupted my routine and threatened to make me late for work.

I caught another bus 30 minutes later than usual. The driver was behind schedule because the traffic was a nightmare. My anxiety level rose as I fixed my eyes straight ahead and worried about the work awaiting me. Then I felt the urge to pray, which I did silently in the crowded bus. Thanking the Lord for the day and seeking God's protection and guidance, I opened my eyes with an entirely new perspective.

Feeling an inner peace that comes only from the presence of God, I looked out of the window of the bus for the first time. The trees were covered with snow, while the entire landscape had been transformed into a pristine white panorama of beauty. I marvelled at God's masterpiece. I also was reminded yet again to turn my worries over to our Lord and to expect through faith that they would be resolved. And they were. I arrived on time and had a good day at the office.

Prayer: *Dear heavenly Father, thank you for lifting problems and worries from our shoulders. By placing them in your hands, we gain peace of heart and mind to focus on all that you have created as a testimony of your love for us. Amen*

Thought for the Day: Prayer changes the way we look at the world around us. *ips. Prayer changes things*

Ken C. Hague (Ontario, Canada)

Stop and Listen

Read Luke 10:38–42

The Lord answered, 'Mary has chosen the right thing, and it will not be taken away from her.'
Luke 10:42 (GNB)

I have been blessed with good health all my life. Recently, though, because of an accident I have not been as active as usual. My inactivity brought to mind a favourite Bible passage—the story of Jesus visiting the home of Martha and Mary.

I had always understood that Jesus chose the home of Martha and Mary because it was well known as a place of fellowship and hospitality, and Jesus wanted as many people as possible to gather there to hear him. I saw Martha as the homemaker who wanted everything perfect for Jesus. I had always thought Jesus should have asked Mary to help Martha in the preparations so that Martha, too, could have sat at his feet and listened.

Because of my new limitations, I have been unable to offer that kind of hospitality to our friends. But reading again this story from Luke's Gospel, I saw the wisdom of just being ready to listen. I can't imagine keeping Jesus waiting while the scones baked or I put away the vacuum!

I am due for some more time of inactivity, but I'm ready to sit at Jesus' feet, to listen and learn from him. That is my main purpose as his follower.

Prayer: *Quiet our hearts, dear Jesus, to hear your words of love and guidance for our lives. Amen*

Thought for the Day: Serving Christ begins with listening to him.

Monica Wood (Garsfontein East, South Africa)

'Pray For Me'

Read Philippians 4:4–7

Carry each other's burdens, and in this way you will fulfil the law of Christ.
Galatians 6:2 (NIV)

My husband called me at work to tell me bad news. Our son had just been expelled from high school because of a drug-related offence. That night, after we had hugged our son and cried and talked with him, my husband and I tried to work out what to do next. Later I e-mailed some close friends to tell them what had happened. 'Pray for us,' I pleaded. I knew we faced a long journey, and I didn't think we could make it without the prayer support of Christian friends.

Over the next three years we learned a lot about surrendering control of our situation to God, about building a more loving relationship with our teenager, about the realities of addiction, about God's love and mercy, and about the importance of praying for others. During the bleakest times, I rested in the knowledge that others were praying for us and in the trust that God would continue working in our lives.

With the help of a 12-step programme and a wonderful counsellor, our son eventually overcame his addiction. I believe that the prayers of others sustained us through this experience, and I hope I will never again take it lightly when someone says, 'Please pray for me.'

Prayer: *Loving God, thank you for the prayers of others that sustain us in our worst times. Help us to be mindful of others' needs and to remember them in prayer. Amen*

Thought for the Day: Praying friends hold us up when we cannot stand on our own.

Anne Leonard Trudel (Tennessee)

PRAYER FOCUS: FAMILIES DEALING WITH ADDICTION

Food for Life

Read John 6:1–13

Jesus said to [the crowd], 'I am the bread of life. Whoever comes to me will never be hungry.'
John 6:35 (NRSV)

After Jesus had fed the huge crowd, when his followers questioned him, he made the great claim, 'I am the bread of life.' Had he been living in Asia today, he might have said, 'I am the rice of life', because rice is a staple of that country's diet. I am glad Jesus didn't say, 'I am the chocolate éclair of life' or 'I am the lemon meringue pie of life'—as lovely as these are. Faith in Jesus Christ is not meant to be a special treat or an occasional luxury. It is a vital ingredient for complete living every day.

Jesus reminded his hearers how the children of Israel were fed on their way to the Promised Land. Six mornings a week, they looked out to discover that God had been faithful, sending manna to feed them. Jesus' comparing himself to bread reminds us of our need to draw sustenance from God each day as we seek to grow and develop our faith.

Prayer: *Gracious God, thank you for your faithfulness to nourish and sustain us as we seek to walk in your ways. We pray as Jesus taught us, saying, 'Our Father which art in heaven, Hallowed be thy name. Thy kingdom come. Thy will be done in earth, as it is in heaven. Give us this day our daily bread. And forgive us our debts, as we forgive our debtors. And lead us not into temptation, but deliver us from evil: For thine is the kingdom, and the power, and the glory, for ever.'* Amen*

Thought for the Day: How can we share the bread of life with those around us?

Link2Life: *Bake something to share with a neighbour.*

Bill Willis (New South Wales, Australia)

PRAYER FOCUS: THOSE WHO DO NOT SEE GOD AT WORK
* Matthew 6:9–13 (KJV)

A Trusting Child

Read Luke 18:15–17

Jesus… said, 'Let the little children come to me, and do not stop them; for it is to such as these that the kingdom of God belongs.'
Luke 18:16 (NRSV)

As physicians, my colleagues and I often work in very poor areas, on hot and sultry days. One morning as we were administering vitamin drops, a child clung tightly to his mother, unwilling to come to us because we were strangers. When his mother chided him, he hugged her more closely; but in obedience, he finally opened his mouth to receive the health-sustaining drops.

When I saw how that child unconditionally trusted his mother, refusing to be separated from her, I remembered the scripture passage in Mark 10:13–16. I thought to myself, 'This is the kind of love that Christ expects us to have.'

Many times when we are faced with problems, instead of coming closer to God we move away. We may even question God's love for us. But we should ask ourselves, 'When times are tough, will I be enough like a child to cling to God, trusting that God knows what's best for me?'

Prayer: *Creator God, help us to love and trust you with the mind and heart of a child. Amen*

Thought for the Day: How is my trust in God like a child's trust in a loving parent?

Beulah Prasad (Bangalore, India)

PRAYER FOCUS: CHILDREN SEPARATED FROM THEIR PARENTS

As Close as a Prayer

Read Psalm 118:19–29
You do not know what a day may bring.
Proverbs 27:1 (NRSV)

Many people carry a diary; we jot down meetings to attend, birthdays or anniversaries, and social events. At the beginning of a week, we look in our diary and assume that we have a clear picture of what we will be doing.

Over time, we become aware of how many unexpected events occur—in our personal life, in our work life, in our community and nation and world. More than 2,000 years ago, a wise person observed, 'You do not know what a day may bring' (Proverbs 27:1). We may be faced with an accident, illness, natural disaster or loss of employment.

But we Christians know that we are not alone in a heartless universe. In every circumstance, every day, God is with us. As the psalmist affirmed, 'This is the day that the Lord has made; let us rejoice and be glad in it' (Psalm 118:24, NRSV). Knowing that God is with us, that the living Christ is as close as a murmured prayer, can take the sting out of heartbreak and give us strength. And an unexpected phone call or letter—or a visit from an old friend—is a real blessing that we didn't know the day might bring.

Prayer: *O God of the present moment, give us open eyes and ears and the will to respond with faith, courage and joy to whatever each day brings. Amen*

Thought for the Day: No matter what my circumstances today, God will be with me.

Fred Cloud (Tennessee)

A Renewed Mind

Read Romans 8:28–37

Do not be conformed to this world, but be transformed by the renewing of your minds, so that you may discern what is the will of God—what is good and acceptable and perfect.
Romans 12:2 (NRSV)

My wife had been fighting a terrible bout of depression and had been unable to work for nearly a year. I felt responsible to provide for our family, so I accepted as much overtime as I could. While she sank deeper into despair, I remained unable to understand or to be empathetic. I convinced myself that I was doing the right thing by working so much. But by doing so I became tired and lonely, even sometimes angry and volatile. I had abandoned my wife and my family, and I had allowed myself to ignore God altogether. Just when I thought life couldn't get any worse, I lost my job.

The next Sunday morning as I sat in worship, a mirror on the organ reflected an image of Jesus carrying a lamb in his arms. At that moment I realised that God had wanted to help all along, but I hadn't allowed it. My feelings of anxiety began to dissipate, and God's grace gave me peace.

With a renewed mind, I knew that it was God's will for our family to begin the healing process. Time off from work to focus all of our attention on God's will for us and on our healing was exactly what our family needed.

Prayer: *Dear heavenly Father, when we feel overwhelmed, help us to remember that your grace overflows into our lives. Open our eyes to see it and our hearts to receive it. Amen*

Thought for the Day: God's will for us is peace.

Earl Fuller (Iowa)

PRAYER FOCUS: FAMILIES DEALING WITH DEPRESSION

Who Are You? Why Are You Here?

Read Matthew 16:13–18

*[Jesus] asked his disciples, 'Who do people say that the Son of Man is? …
But who do you say that I am?'*
Matthew 16:13, 15 (NRSV)

There is something quite comforting about knowing who someone is, don't you think? Recently, I spent some time at a weekday
playgroup in my town. During my visit, I observed and chatted with
three-to-five-year-olds who only wanted to know two things about
me: 'Who are you? Why are you here?' Once they were satisfied with
my answers, they either went about their business or talked about
what they were doing. But I kept thinking about what they wanted
to know.

These questions are critical to all of us in our journey as we seek
to understand who we are. What is our identity as Christians? The
Bible reminds us that the answers may not be obvious. Those who
did not know Jesus well mistook him for someone else; but Simon
Peter, who spent much time with Jesus, identified him as the Messiah and followed him.

How is God calling us? Where, why and whom are we to serve?
As we seek these answers through prayer, meditation and conversations with God, we will find God leading us into serving others in
ways that will show us who we and Christ are.

Prayer: *Loving God, open our eyes to see where you are calling us to
serve in your name. Help us to live patiently into your answers to all our
questions. Amen*

Thought for the Day: Serving others in God's name reveals to us
who we are.

Melanie Gordon (Tennessee)

Small Packages

Read Ephesians 3:14–21
[The Lord] will bless everyone who honours him, the great and the small alike.
Psalm 115:13 (GNB)

As often happens for me, two small incidents converged within a short space of time to bring an insight about God. Early one day, I had picked up a tiny, fallen birch leaf. Carefully, I held in my hand its brittle autumn beauty; and I observed that the leaf was no less resplendent than its larger companions scattered across the grass or still parachuting from the trees. They all shared a family likeness. Later that day, we picked the last of our small crop of tomatoes. Biting into the smallest, we relished all the glorious flavour common to the rest of the crop, even the biggest. The reminder from scripture was Paul's phrase, 'filled with all the fullness of God' (Ephesians 3:19, NRSV).

In spite of their size, both the tiny leaf and the small tomato were fully what God made them to be. In Christian experience, every person—regardless of importance, ability or achievement—can be filled with God's spirit and share all the beauty and flavour of Christ. As we come to know Christ's love more and more deeply, we can be 'filled with all the fullness of God' and by doing so, show God to others.

Prayer: *Holy Spirit, fill our lives with the knowledge of your love. Amen*

Thought for the Day: The great love of God often comes in small packages.

Colin D. Harbach (Cumbria, England)

PRAYER FOCUS: THOSE WHO FEEL INSIGNIFICANT

Just a Playhouse?

Read 1 Thessalonians 5:9–18

Let us come into [God's] presence with thanksgiving.
Psalm 95:2 (NRSV)

A few days before Thanksgiving, my eight-year-old granddaughter, Kate, took me to the edge of the woods where she had begun to construct her 'playhouse'. She proudly showed me the various 'rooms' and then enlisted my help to make a roof by wedging long sticks between trees. As she brought me smaller branches and pine needles to place across the top, she was delighted with this rag-tag mess. I was pleased that she could find joy amid the financial trials her family was having since the company her father worked for had gone out of business.

Then, the day before Thanksgiving, I saw a picture from Darfur. A refugee family huddled under a makeshift stick dwelling as flimsy as Kate's playhouse. I remembered that the Bible says we are to give thanks in everything—not necessarily for everything, but to live with gratitude no matter what (see 1 Thessalonians 5:18).

I do not know what desperate refugees give thanks for, but they remind me that struggling people all over the world need my prayers. In addition, their plight reminded me that I need to pay more attention to my attitude. I want to thank God for whatever I can and 'take delight in the small joys of life'.

Prayer: *Dear God, forgive us for grumbling. Remind us of your love and teach us the peace that comes from a grateful heart. Amen*

Thought for the Day: We can replace grumbling with gratitude.

Link2Life: *Find out how you can help overseas projects working with refugees.*

Dolly Dickinson (North Carolina)

Acknowledging the Giver

Read Psalm 65

Every generous act of giving, with every perfect gift, is from above, coming down from the Father of lights, with whom there is no variation or shadow due to change.

James 1:17 (NRSV)

One of our treasured keepsakes is a homemade table decoration: a turkey made of feathers, pipe cleaners, silver paper and sticking-out eyes. It was created and given to us several Thanksgivings ago by our niece when she was very young, and it has graced our table during the holidays ever since.

Over time, this turkey has become rather dilapidated. Still, every year, we get it out and set it on the holiday table—not because of the qualities of the turkey, but because of our love for our niece and the memory of her joy in presenting this gift to us.

We have so much to give thanks for that we cannot possibly name it all. But when we pause to acknowledge the Giver of all these good gifts, a real spirit of thanksgiving rises within us. When we view our many blessings in light of our relationship with God, life takes on a true sense of wholeness, and giving thanks becomes more than a holiday tradition. It becomes our natural response to God who, in infinite love, has given us all that is good in our lives.

Prayer: *Dear God, give us truly thankful hearts. May we live each day in awareness of your generosity. Amen*

Thought for the Day: All good gifts still come from God!

Michael W. Lowry (Ohio)

Overflowing Comfort

Read 2 Corinthians 1:3–7

Just as the sufferings of Christ flow over into our lives, so also through Christ our comfort overflows.
2 Corinthians 1:5 (NIV)

I lead worship at a homeless shelter. Jeff, a new resident, seemed particularly anxious and before we began the service, raised two heartfelt questions: 'Why is this happening to me? What am I doing here?' Despite his faith, Jeff was unsure whether these questions even had answers. Several of us shared our personal stories and the passage above to encourage Jeff and to reassure him that his life is valuable to God.

God has fitted each of us with unique gifts and a purpose, but trials come into our lives nonetheless. As followers of Christ, we will surely share in his suffering. But we also share in the comfort of Christ. Then, as Christ's comfort eases our trials, that comfort can overflow from our lives into the lives of others. When I was diagnosed with cancer, God provided numerous people to encourage me prior to my surgery. Then as I recovered, men who anxiously awaited the same surgery seemed to cross my path. I was able to share with them the comfort Christ had brought to me. Even in our times of greatest pain, God provides us with a message to give and someone who needs to hear it.

Prayer: *Lord God, help us to let you use our struggles to bring comfort to others. Amen*

Thought for the Day: Our sufferings can become opportunities to help others.

Link2Life: *Can you volunteer to work with homeless people?*

Dan Nelson (North Carolina)

PRAYER FOCUS: SOMEONE ANXIOUS ABOUT SURGERY

Consequences

Read Matthew 6:7–15

Jesus said, 'If you forgive others their trespasses, your heavenly Father will also forgive you.'
Matthew 6:14 (NRSV)

Opening the back door, I was confronted by an angry neighbour. Her voice drowned out the sounds of our children playing happily in her garden. She stood, fists clenched, eyes blazing, mouth spewing accusations against my children and me. My hand itched to slap her face. Instead, I called the boys in and closed the door.

Anger rose within me like a boiling cauldron at such unwarranted abuse. But instead of handing it to God, I held on to it, allowing it to fester and taint my life. Then one day Jesus brought me to my knees with these words from the Lord's Prayer: 'Forgive us our trespasses as we forgive those who trespass against us.' I felt an ice-cold arrow targeting my simmering anger.

My family had had to live with the consequences of that anger. I had lost a relationship with a neighbour, and the children lost their playmate—until God helped me to see the truth. If we do not hand over our anger, hatred and pride to God, those emotions can destroy our lives. I thank God for a lesson learned—the hard way.

Prayer: *Dear Lord, forgive us when we hold tight to harmful emotions. We are good at rationalising and justifying our actions. Help us to let go of our pride and hurt, to focus on others rather than ourselves, and to see beyond hurtful words. Amen*

Thought for the Day: Refusing to forgive harms us from the inside out.

Julia Cutting (East Yorkshire, England)

Christmas Revealed

Read Revelation 1:4–8

Grace to you and peace from him who is and who was and who is to come.

Revelation 1:4 (NRSV)

'Grace to you and peace from him who is and who was and who is to come.' In this greeting lies a reminder that God is eternal. In this greeting is a reminder that harmony has been restored between God and humanity through Christ, a reminder that God remains steadfast even in the midst of life's most trying and terrible days.

So what does this have to do with Christmas? It is tempting to make Christmas into a warm fuzzy tale about a baby born in a humble stable, surrounded by adoring witnesses singing songs of praise under a starlit sky. But this passage from Revelation reminds us of whom this child will grow to be, of where his birth will ultimately lead—a glimpse into the mystery of God's purpose at Christmas.

This child will bear faithful and reliable witness to God's self-giving love—good news for a weary world. This child will make kings and rulers tremble and bring nations and empires to their knees!

At the core of Christmas is the One who is the 'Alpha and the Omega', the beginning and the end. The God 'who is and who was and who is to come, the Almighty' is about to come and live among us (see John 1:14).

Prayer: *Reveal to us, O God, in the story of the Christ Child, the mystery of your eternal purpose. Show us the power of your love, and make known in our world the Good News that will bring us peace. Amen*

Thought for the Day: Christmas is good news—from beginning to end!

F. Richard Garland (Rhode Island)

Clothed by Christ

Read Ephesians 6:10–17

Above all, clothe yourselves with love, which binds everything together in perfect harmony.
Colossians 3:14 (NRSV)

My granddaughter loves to choose which clothes she wears each day. She reminds me of how my friend and I used to go to clothes shops simply to look at the new designs and try a few things on. We did not have any money to buy anything, and the assistants knew this. However, they understood our feelings and allowed us to play our dressing-up game. Each time we tried on a new outfit and looked at ourselves in the mirror, we felt we were looking at someone from another world. How quickly we were transformed! Even then we understood how much clothes can say about a person.

Many years have gone by since then. On 7 October 1985, I accepted Christ as my Saviour. I acquired a new life and became a different person. Now I understand that our best and most important clothing is spiritual: 'As God's chosen ones, holy and beloved, clothe yourselves with compassion, kindness, humility, meekness and patience' (Colossians 3:12, NRSV). This clothing transforms our whole life and all that is within us. The clothing God wants us to wear is purity, modesty, humility and, above all, love. This spiritual clothing never frays; in fact, it becomes more beautiful every day when we honour the One who gives it to us.

Prayer: *Lord Jesus Christ, as we dress each morning, remind us to put on love so that we honour you in all we do. Amen*

Thought for the Day: We're never fully dressed until we put on love.

Lyudmila Garbuzova (Moscow, Russia)

PRAYER FOCUS: NEW CHRISTIANS

Interruption or Opportunity?

Read Matthew 25:31–40

Job said, 'I was a father to the needy; I took up the case of the stranger.'
Job 29:16 (NIV)

My morning began very early with a phone call that required a trip to a distant hospital to visit a seriously ill church member. The rest of my day as a pastor was filled with pastoral visits, meetings, paperwork, phone calls, and, finally, teaching the evening Bible study. The long day made me look forward to going home and resting.

As I walked back to my house I was greeted by two strangers sitting on my front steps. My initial thoughts were, 'What now?' The strangers greeted me with a request for assistance. They were a homeless couple travelling to another town. They needed overnight lodging and a meal. In my tiredness I silently prayed, 'Lord Jesus, let me see your face in these people. Let me serve you.' I arranged for accommodation and a meal for the travellers. As I returned home again late that night, I felt the presence of Christ near me. Christ had been with those homeless travellers, and Christ had been with me in my tiredness.

Christ comes to us in the unexpected and in the interruptions. Once again I had the opportunity to see my Christian service not as interruption or obligation but as an opportunity to be in the real presence of the risen Christ.

Prayer: *God of compassion, give us the strength and resolve to help those around us who have a need that we can meet. Amen*

Thought for the Day: Interruptions can be opportunities to minister with Christ.

Jerry W. Krueger (Texas)

Comfort My People

Read Isaiah 40:1–8

Comfort, O comfort my people, says your God.

Isaiah 40:1 (NRSV)

As I walked my dog one cold December evening, my boots squeaked in the snow. Drawing near our village graveyard, I was mystified to see a soft glow of lights in its far corner. I decided to investigate. The snow almost reached the top of my boots as I carefully slid down the small incline toward the glow. Next to the grave of a man who had recently died was a small Christmas tree, decorated with white Christmas lights.

I imagined his widow reminiscing about Christmases past as she placed this tree by his grave. I couldn't help but think about the contrast between my home, brimming with Christmas anticipation, and that family with an empty seat at the table. This season of comfort and joy can also be a time of sadness and grief.

As we celebrate the birth of Jesus, we remember that Christ came to offer comfort to the broken-hearted and hope to the lonely. Those Christmas lights reminded me to be especially aware of people in need of God's love and compassion.

Prayer: *Dear God, today and every day we celebrate Emmanuel, that you are always with us. Help us to share your hope with those who need it most as we pray, 'Father, hallowed be your name, your kingdom come. Give us each day our daily bread. Forgive us our sins, for we also forgive everyone who sins against us. And lead us not into temptation.'* * Amen

Thought for the Day: How can I share Christ's love with someone who is bereaved?

Link2Life: *Share your Christmas celebration with someone who would otherwise be alone.*

Susan J. Foster (Connecticut)

PRAYER FOCUS: THOSE MOURNING IN THIS SEASON OF JOY

* Luke 11:2–4 (NIV)

Caring for Widows

Read Psalm 146:5–9

Religion that is pure and undefiled before God, the Father, is this: to care for orphans and widows in their distress.
James 1:27 (NRSV)

Early last year I spent a quiet week at a Christian retreat centre near the Scottish border. There were only a few guests, but among them was Berna, whose husband Jim had died within the previous two months. Berna had given up her job to nurse Jim during the last year of his life. When we met she was full of grief. Before we parted we exchanged addresses and promised to write. Over the year that followed we wrote back and forth regularly. Berna spoke freely about her dear Jim, and I felt free to ask questions about him. She told me that writing to me and receiving my letters was healing for her.

The Bible urges us to care for widows and orphans, and I'm sure this extends to others we know who are suffering some loss. It doesn't take much to show that we care. Some people visit and offer home-baked foods, while others take flowers. Some send postcards. Some send little gifts. These are the sorts of things that say we remember, small acts that offer a bright spot in an otherwise sad day. These loving gestures make a difference.

Prayer: *Dear Lord, help us to give generously of our time to those who grieve. Show us how we can make a difference. Amen*

Thought for the Day: Sorrowing people need a friend.

Link2Life: *Offer a word of encouragement or an act of kindness for someone lonely or grieving the loss of a loved one.*

Elinor Jones (West Lothian, Scotland)

Who Wants to be Free?

Read Matthew 8:28–34

Do not be wise in your own eyes; fear the Lord, and turn away from evil.
Proverbs 3:7 (NRSV)

I was brought up in a church with unorthodox views about Jesus. When I returned from college, I used the Bible and the church's history to point out the difficulties of my family's faith. My uncle became aggravated and said, 'Why are you telling us this?'

I said, 'Because it's the truth. "You will know the truth, and the truth will make you free"' (John 8:32, NRSV).

He replied, 'Who wants to be free?'

My uncle was not the first one to adopt that stance. Matthew tells how Jesus cast a legion of demons out of two men. What happened next was as remarkable. The witnesses to the miracle ran into town and 'told the whole story about what had happened to the demoniacs. Then the whole town came out to meet Jesus; and when they saw him, they begged him to leave their neighbourhood' (Matthew 8:33–34, NRSV).

The scripture passage does not say what the people believed that was more important to them than the truth and power of Jesus. But excessive attachment to any tradition or ideology can divert us from a living relationship with God. The story in Matthew reminds me eagerly to raise my hand when Jesus asks, 'Who wants to be free?'

Prayer: *Dear God, give us faith in the truth of Jesus Christ. Amen*

Thought for the Day: What fears, desires or ideas stand between me and God?

Kent H. Roberts (Texas)

PRAYER FOCUS: THOSE WHO HOLD FAST TO FALSE BELIEFS

Christmas Card Snow

Read Psalm 34:1–10

O taste and see that the Lord is good; happy are those who take refuge in him.

Psalm 34:8 (NRSV)

As a young girl growing up in the warm Mississippi Delta, I would sit out on our front steps in the wintertime and pray for snow. Though we did get a light dusting here and there, the closest thing I ever saw to a really good snow came on the front of glittery Christmas cards. Longingly, I would turn the cards this way and that in the light, imagining what a big snow would look like on my front lawn.

When I grew older, beautiful, bright Christmas cards came in the post, and in my more grown-up mind I would think, 'Why, that's just glitter. Snow doesn't really look like that.' Later, when I was married, we moved to a Midwestern city. When the first big snow was forecast, I couldn't wait. One night it happened; snow showered down. Much to my amazement, I saw that the snow really did sparkle like a thousand little jewels. The Christmas-card images that had stirred my imagination were accurate.

How like my spiritual walk that discovery has been! As a child I believed in God but had never really *experienced* God. Later I wondered if God really was everything I had been taught. Then I found the truth: that the God I had believed in as a child was even more wonderful than anything I could have imagined. I discovered how much God really loves us, and how, like the glittering snow, God showers us with light—and bountiful, glittering love.

Prayer: *Dear Lord, thank you for the mercy, love and tenderness you shower on us. May we always be amazed by your goodness to us. Amen*

Thought for the Day: God delights in showering us with love.

Mary Hughes (Missouri)

PRAYER FOCUS: NEW DISCOVERIES ABOUT GOD'S LOVE

Only a Shepherd?

Read Luke 2:8–20

'How beautiful are the feet of those who bring good news!'
Romans 10:15 (NRSV)

Who gets to be Mary? Joseph? One of the kings? Those questions were always asked when I was directing the Christmas nativity play at church. Mary and Joseph were the most prestigious roles in the play, and the kings got to wear fancy robes and crowns. The shepherds didn't seem all that important. They just wrapped towels around their heads and watched. They were part of a larger group; they dressed alike and blended into the scenery. No one wanted to be a shepherd.

But I don't think the shepherds in the Christmas story get enough recognition. They were, after all, the first ones the angels told about the birth of Jesus Christ. They were among the first to see the baby Jesus. And they were the ones who first told the good news to others. The lowly shepherds had an important role to play in Jesus' story.

In the same way, God has an important role for each of us to play. Whether kings or shepherds, we are all called to tell others about our Saviour and to proclaim the good news of his resurrection.

Prayer: *God of all people, help us to be the shepherds of today, glorifying and praising you and telling others about Jesus Christ. Amen*

Thought for the Day: No matter what our station in life, we can witness to the good news of God's love.

Xavia Arndt Sheffield (Maryland)

My Priorities

Read Mark 13:31–37

Is not this the fast that I choose… to share your bread with the hungry, and bring the homeless poor into your house?
Isaiah 58:6–7 (NRSV)

I had overslept. There was no time to read The Upper Room that morning. I had to get to the office early in order to send a Christmas parcel to Paris. On my way there, I walked past an Orthodox church where an elderly lady standing outside asked me for some money. I didn't stop; I was far more concerned about how long I would have to wait at the post office during this busy time of year.

Before going to bed that night, I finally decided to have my devotional time. The meditation for that day was written by a woman who had driven past a homeless man for several days, and she was feeling troubled by seeing his situation. She finally decided to pack up some food to give to him—but when she arrived at the street corner where he had always been, he was no longer there.

I realised immediately that my priorities for the day had been wrong. If I had read that meditation in the morning, as I usually do, my day—and the elderly woman's day—might have turned out very differently. I passed by an opportunity for God to use me to help someone in need.

Prayer: *God of love, give us this day our daily bread. Help us to be aware that those around us need daily bread too. Amen*

Thought for the Day: Would my priorities for today please God?

Link2Life: *Prepare a package of imperishable food items. Give it to someone in need as you commute or travel.*

The Russian girl.

Nicola Vidamour (Pskov, Russia)

God with Us

Read Psalm 121:1–8

I lift up my eyes to the hills—from where will my help come?
Psalm 121:1 (NRSV)

Election day in Kenya was 27 December 2007. A lot of tension surrounded the election, and speculation about which of the two main presidential contestants would emerge the winner. Support for the candidates reflected loyalty to their different tribes. The announcement of the winner was slow in coming, and even after the announcement, reactions were mixed. People raised questions about whether the process had been free and fair.

I am of the Luhya tribe from the city of Kakamega, and I was living in a town on the outskirts of Nairobi at the time of the election. Fights erupted in the city, and a few killings were reported. Our neighbours, who were of a different tribe, were issuing threats and dropping threatening notes on our doorstep. I decided to take my wife and children to a town that I felt was safer. But one of my neighbours, who was of my tribe, remained. When I asked him to move with us he simply said, 'The Lord will protect me.'

When the unrest ended, I visited the place and found him safe. I learned a lesson: God is with us at all times and through all the circumstances of our lives. Whether we flee or stay, God is faithful. God will use our words, our decisions and the steps we take to reach out to us.

Prayer: *Dear God, you use all that we do for your purposes. Teach us to rely on you in all the circumstances of our lives. Amen*

Thought for the Day: God is with us.

Manase Shiyuka (Nairobi, Kenya)

PRAYER FOCUS: COUNTRIES FACING POLITICAL UNREST

My Home Town

Read Philippians 3:10–14

The one thing I do… is to forget what is behind me and do my best to reach what is ahead.

Philippians 3:13 (GNB)

I was determined to celebrate this Christmas well. I would not rush; I would put love into it. And to my surprise, it worked. Never before had I enjoyed Advent so much. But as Christmas Day drew near, something was missing. I was strangely drawn to visit the graves of my parents. I felt unfinished business between them and me. Our relationships had not been what I wanted them to be. As I continued to recall my home town and the painful past, I became convinced that I could not go back.

However, the urge to return continued to compel me. So on Christmas Eve, I set out. The closer I got, the more uneasy and nervous I became. 'How can something that's over upset me so?' I asked myself. As I reached the outskirts of the town, I stopped to think. Finally the answer came to me: I was holding on to something that I needed to forgive. 'Father,' I prayed, 'I want to forgive it all, myself included. I choose to let it go.'

Driving into town, I expected the ugly, rundown little place that I remembered. But it wasn't there. In its place was a radiant, friendly town. The shops, the decorations, the pavements—I remembered every detail. 'This is *my* town,' I said proudly, tears streaming down my face. God was helping me to forgive and to put to rest my struggle with the past.

Prayer: *God of peace, help me let go of yesterday so I can experience the fullness of life that you offer today. Amen*

Thought for the Day: Christmas is a good time to forgive past hurts.

Carolyn Caldwell (South Carolina)

Being Models

Read 1 Thessalonians 1:1–10
We proclaim to you what we have seen and heard, so that you also may have fellowship with us. And our fellowship is with the Father and with his Son, Jesus Christ.
1 John 1:3 (NIV)

'I've organised a dinner for you,' Maureen said to me with excited anticipation. I was a visitor to the area; and on Saturday night, I met with six other women to enjoy food and fun and to talk about the love of God in our lives.

What a joy it was to arrive at church the next morning and find a group of people I already knew! Instead of being the awkward new-comer, nervous about being isolated and worried about what might happen, I was able to greet others and to relate to them comfortably with a sense of belonging. During subsequent meetings and a women's conference, I built a network of friends.

Maureen had used hospitality to express her love and to help her church grow. Wasn't that a good model for me, too? Shouldn't I be asking God to show me ways to draw people into fellowship with our group and with Christ?

Maureen didn't preach a sermon. She demonstrated her love for and hope in Christ by putting her faith into action.

Prayer: *Dear God, please help us to draw others into a warm and accepting fellowship with you. Amen*

Thought for the Day: How many Christians would there be if all believers followed my example?

Link2Life: *Help your church find ways to welcome newcomers.*

Marjorie Moody (Queensland, Australia)

Lighting the Way

Read Romans 8:38–39
Your word is a lamp to my feet and a light to my path.
Psalm 119:105 (NRSV)

At 4:45, I left the house for my morning run. I live in the country, and the sources of light for my early morning runs are the moon, the stars and lights from farmhouses. I had looked forward to running in the light of a full moon, but clouds blocked the light. I was more than a little disappointed. Being plunged into darkness left me with the dual challenge of seeing where I was running and making myself seen by early morning commuters.

Toward the end of my run, a break in the clouds allowed me to see the moon. It not only made the sky a beautiful patchwork of light and dark but also lit the way for me.

When we find ourselves plunged into darkness, we often feel trapped, separated, lost, fretful, anxious and alone. We don't know where we are, and we are unable to get where we want to go. We need a guiding light.

That morning's glorious moonlight reminded me that we are never alone. In all circumstances, God walks with us in love, care and concern. Even when darkness in our lives causes us to feel lost or disoriented, God searches us out and provides light to guide us home.

Prayer: *Dear God, help us to understand that in the dark times you are with us, guiding, comforting and encouraging us through your word. Thank you for protection and for the light of your love. Amen*

Thought for the Day: God's word is light in our darkness.

Cole Warner (Wisconsin)

Comfort for God's People

Read Luke 24: 30–52

[The travellers] asked each other, 'Were not our hearts burning within us while he talked with us on the road and opened the Scriptures to us?'
Luke 24:32 (NIV)

I had just walked into a shop in December. Christmas decorations were everywhere; Christmas carols played. As I watched the shoppers, I realised that this was supposed to be a season of joy. But I was filled with worries and anxiety.

It had been an eventful year. I had hoped to celebrate and enjoy it, but I had had to deal with challenges one after another. I faced with fear an uncertain future, like the two disciples on their way to Emmaus as they discussed the events of the previous three days. But then Someone joined them.

With downcast faces, they revealed their disappointment. They had hoped that Jesus would be the one to save Israel, but his crucifixion had left them troubled about the future. Then their hope was restored when Jesus revealed himself to them, and they rushed back to Jerusalem to be with the other disciples.

Like those downcast disciples, in being reunited with those who love me—my parents, brothers and sisters—I found strength to face my future. The joy of being with my family took away my fears and worries. This reminded me that God's hand is ever-present to comfort us as we gather with other believers. We are never alone, however fearsome our circumstances may seem to be.

Prayer: *Loving God, thank you for comfort when we feel fearful, anxious and worried about what the future holds for us. Amen*

Thought for the Day: In every challenge we face, God wills only good for each of us.

Philip Polo (Nairobi, Kenya)

PRAYER FOCUS: THOSE ANXIOUS DURING THE CHRISTMAS SEASON

Best Gift of All

Read John 3:16–21

God so loved the world that he gave his one and only Son, that whoever believes in him shall not perish but have eternal life.
John 3:16 (NIV)

Like most people, I love gifts. I love to receive them, and I love to give them. I start getting excited about Christmas in September or even earlier. I can't wait to decide what I will give the members of my family. Shall I make something or buy something for each person? Thinking about the gifts I will give my grandchildren is so much fun for me! I can't wait for them to open their gifts, and I love the way their faces light up when they like what I have given.

I wonder if that was how God felt when giving 'his one and only Son'? When Jesus was born, was God watching to see if we would be excited? Was God sad when we didn't seem to appreciate the gift of Jesus? I know I'm disappointed when my children or grandchildren don't like the gifts I give; but I'm thrilled when they love what I've picked out for them. I hope God is thrilled to see that I love Jesus and that I am happy for the gift God gave me.

No matter how great the gifts I give my children and grandchildren, nothing I give can come close to God's great gift of Jesus. Beginning with my family, I want to tell those around me the good news of Jesus Christ so they can receive the best gift ever given.

Prayer: *Thank you, God, for the gift of Jesus. Amen*

Thought for the Day: Jesus is the best gift ever given to us.

Link2Life: *Total up what you usually spend on Christmas gifts. How does this compare to what you give to God in a month?*

Susie Hoffmann (Ohio)

A Community of Prayer

Read Philippians 1:3–11

I do not cease to give thanks for you as I remember you in my prayers.
Ephesians 1:16 (NRSV)

One of the foundations of Christian community is prayer. We pray for our country and its leaders, for the church and for the members of the community. Prayer time is a key part of most worship services. We have the opportunity every week to pray for someone in the community who is ill or grieving.

However, there is always the danger that these prayers may become automatic, just another element of the service. Speaking from personal experience, however, I have discovered that these prayers we pray for others are an integral part of the healing process.

I learned this recently when I underwent major brain surgery. This was the first operation I had ever experienced, and it really scared me at first. Then I learned that fellow Christians from several churches were praying for me. I was amazed! I went into the operating theatre with no fear, supported by the knowledge that the outcome was safely in God's hands. The operation was a success, physically, emotionally and spiritually. I am grateful for the faith and concern of all who cared enough to pray for me.

Now when I am asked to pray for somebody, I do it with gusto! I know that God hears and answers our prayers.

Prayer: *Dear God, you are always with us, especially during times of fear and distress. Help us to sense your comfort and your calming presence when we reach for you in prayer. Amen*

Thought for the Day: Who in my community needs my prayers today?

Kenneth E. Hill (Virginia)

A Promise of Protection

Read Psalm 91
God said, 'I will be with you.'
Exodus 3:12 (NIV)

Recently I went on a journey far from home. I travelled alone across the country for eight days. I visited several cities and spent time with friends along the way. Still, my parents were concerned about me. They expressed a real need to talk to me every day without fail.

Though many of my parents' friends reassured them I could take care of myself, my parents were uncertain about my well-being when they couldn't be near me. Because I was so far away from them, in their minds my welfare seemed in constant jeopardy.

But God is always with us and does not want harm to come to us. God's promise of protection, coupled with paying attention to our inner voices and common sense, keeps us from harm. I'm sure my parents would be surprised to hear that every night on my trek I prayed for safety and that my parents' fears and worries would subside. If my journey taught me anything, it is that God is with us every step of the way, no matter where we go.

Prayer: *Dear God, please help to ease our minds in an already troubled and dangerous world. Remind us daily that your love abounds to shield us from harm. Amen*

Thought for the Day: How can I help guide those who need direction?

Megan Stafford (Tennessee)

Being Chosen

Read John 15:12–17

Jesus said, 'You did not choose me but I chose you.'
John 15:16 (NRSV)

When I was eight years old, I went to sign up for elementary-school basketball. We were told to sit in the gym while several older boys chose teams. I grew up on a farm. As a kid from the country, I did not know any of the city kids who were choosing teams. My knowledge of basketball and of the proper attire was nil. I didn't have a pair of trainers, so I sat in the gym in my stocking feet. I wore big, thick glasses and had a slight build. I was not a first-round choice; nor was I chosen in the second, the third or even the tenth round. Finally, out of about 50 players, the choice came down to me and one other boy. I prayed, 'Let them choose me', but my prayer went unanswered. I was the last person chosen. By default, the team had to take me. The experience was humiliating, and my basketball career was short-lived.

As an adult, I was glad to read Jesus' welcoming words about choosing his team of disciples. With me in my stocking feet, wearing my big glasses and having little to recommend me, Jesus invited me to be a member of his team. It was an experience for which I will be forever grateful. And Christ does this for each of us!

Prayer: *Friend and Redeemer, thank you for choosing us to be part of your team in spite of our limitations. Make us more than conquerors through your benevolent coaching. Amen*

Thought for the Day: God chooses each of us.

Ronald Wunsch (Indiana)

A Sure Elevation

Read Luke 19:1–10

[Zacchaeus] wanted to see who Jesus was, but being a short man he could not, because of the crowd. So he ran ahead and climbed a sycamore-fig tree to see him, since Jesus was coming that way.
Luke 19:3–4 (NIV)

Though I am not physically short, my spiritual vision has often been poor because of the short stature of my faith. Just as the tree provided Zacchaeus with the necessary elevation for a clear view of Christ, so have many individuals been the 'tree' for me in my quest to see Jesus. Ministers have spoken words I needed to hear. Parents have cautioned me when my tendency was to be careless. Christian friends have had the faithful discipline that I lacked and have witnessed to me with their lives faithfully lived. Ministers 'walked the walk' as well as they talked it. My wife's compassion has served as a pattern for how to deal with a hardened heart. My children love me even when I am not lovable. Even the love shown by non-believers has reminded me of God's immeasurable grace. All these have been 'trees' in my life that have given me a clearer view of Christ.

When we doubt our effectiveness in our Christian walk, we can remember that we may be, each of us, a tree for someone. What an awesome privilege and responsibility each of us has in helping others to see Jesus!

Prayer: *Dear Lord, help us be willing to live faithfully so that others can have a clear view of you and your love. Amen*

Thought for the Day: Each one of us can help others see Jesus.

K. Jackson Peevy (Alabama)

Up and Out

Read Psalm 40:1–5
[The Lord] lifted me out of the slimy pit, out of the mud and mire; he set my feet on a rock and gave me a firm place to stand.
Psalm 40:2 (NIV)

I am an inmate in a maximum-security prison. I live in the Restrictive Housing Unit, often and aptly referred to as 'The Hole'. Isolated from the general population, it is a lonely and despairing place, void of any signs of comfort or compassion. I am imprisoned by its seemingly impenetrable walls.

At one time, however, I was every bit as imprisoned even though no walls surrounded me. Sin and its accompanying entanglements had plunged me deep into a pit of spiritual darkness. But like the psalmist I cried out to God and found that the walls of that pit were not impenetrable. God lifted me up and out of it.

Even in 'the hole' I see Bibles and Christian literature, catch glimpses of inmates praying, and hear prisoners calling out to speak with the chaplain.

No matter how deep in the mud and mire of sin we may find ourselves, no matter how isolated, helpless and hopeless we might feel, God can hear us, lift us up and out, and give us a firm place to stand.

Prayer: *O Lord, no matter how deep our troubles are may we look to you for help, for deliverance from destruction and despair and all that imprisons us. Thank you, Lord, for being our refuge and salvation. Amen*

Thought for the Day: No pit is deep enough to put us beyond God's reach.

Charles P. Axe (Pennsylvania)

PRAYER FOCUS: THOSE IN PRISON

The Aroma of Christ

Read John 13:1–17

We are to God the aroma of Christ among those who are being saved and those who are perishing.
2 Corinthians 2:15 (NIV)

My daughter, Andrea, arrived at the hospital at about 5:00 a.m. on the morning of my granddaughter's birth. Fifteen minutes later, a nurse came to the door of my daughter's room where she and my son-in-law, Tim, were waiting and said, 'There is someone here to see you.' The visitor was an 80-year-old member of the church where Tim serves as a youth leader.

This church member spent the next several minutes praying with Andrea and Tim about the birth that was coming. When he left, the nurse in charge asked who he was.

Tim answered, 'He is one of our church members.'

She said, 'I knew it. I just knew it. He had the smell of Jesus all over him!'

What the nurse didn't know was that two days before, this same man had brought over food that he had prepared himself for us to have over the next few busy days. We all had come to know that he had 'the aroma of Christ' (2 Corinthians 2:15, NIV) about him. Being good news to others can often open doors later for sharing the good news of salvation.

Prayer: *Dear God, forgive our selfishness. Help us to focus on the needs of others, to be good news to others before we tell them the good news. In Jesus' name we pray. Amen*

Thought for the Day: How can I be 'the aroma of Christ' to someone today?

Andy Baker (Tennessee)

Thanking the Source

Read Luke 17:11–19

One of [the men who had leprosy]… came back, praising God in a loud voice. He threw himself at Jesus' feet and thanked him.
Luke 17:15–16 (NIV)

After Sunday school, my colleague and I gave bags of sweets to our pupils and wished them a Merry Christmas. The children happily received their gifts, said thanks, and began eating as they walked away. We were preparing to leave when one boy shyly approached and asked for a bag for his disabled brother, who was walking behind him, with difficulty. The fragile boy called out, 'Teacher, please wait for me.' His brother ran to him and said, 'I already thanked her for both of us. Here, thank me instead for getting your share.' The boy took the gift but still made his way toward me.

'I want to thank you myself because you are the one who really gave us the gifts,' he said and lovingly kissed my hand. His words and sincere way of expressing gratitude reminded me of the Samaritan leper whom Jesus healed. Then I asked myself, 'How many of us Christians sometimes behave like the other nine lepers—slow to say "Thank you!" for gifts? And when we do feel grateful, whom do we thank first and most?'

While it is good to thank the people who help us, shouldn't we thank our loving God even more? After all, the Bible teaches us that everything and everyone belongs to God (see Psalm 24:1). We can live each day in praise and thanksgiving to our generous and loving God, the source of all good gifts (see Psalm 103:2–4; James 1:17).

Prayer: *Giver of all good gifts, thank you for your unfailing love. Fill us with gratitude for all you give us. Amen*

Thought for the Day: We glorify God when we give thanks.

Vilma May A. Fuentes (Davao City, Philippines)

God Knows Us

Read Psalm 139:1–5
The psalmist wrote, 'Even before a word is on my tongue, O Lord, you know it completely.'
Psalm 139:4 (NRSV)

I fondly recall the close neighbourhoods of small towns in Kentucky when I was a child. Everyone knew everyone else. The children attended the same primary school. Neighbours brought food when someone was ill, and parents kept an eye each other's children.

Today the culture has changed. We may nod to our neighbours but don't engage them in conversation. Our work colleagues may know a little about us but not the details of our personal life.

Whether others know us or not, a universal truth is that God knows everything about us. The Lord of the universe knows our most intimate thoughts and the details of our heart. Some couples, after a lengthy period of marriage, can complete each other's sentences. The psalmist tells us that 'even before a word is on my tongue, O Lord, you know it completely' (Psalm 139:4, NRSV). What an awesome yet scary thought! God knows our thoughts and actions and offers us protection on our way.

In every situation we face today, we can rejoice that God protects, guides and loves. God knows us completely and loves us. As children of God, we can celebrate God's blessing and rejoice in God's active involvement in our daily lives.

Prayer: *Dear heavenly Father, we rejoice that you know our thoughts even before we think them. Help us every day to sense your presence, guidance and love. Amen*

Thought for the Day: God knows us completely and loves us anyway.

W. Terry Whalin (Arizona)

Even Us Sinners

Read 1 John 4:7–21

God demonstrates his own love for us in this: while we were still sinners, Christ died for us.

Romans 5:8 (NIV)

My daughters are six and four years old. The elder daughter often takes things from her younger sister and bullies her. I worry that when she goes to school, she will treat her classmates the same way. Though at times I find my older daughter's behaviour trying, of course I still love her.

In a similar way, God loves each of us even when we behave badly, never withholding love from us. The more we commit sin, the more God's grace abounds (see Romans 5:20). God never gives up on us, Instead, in limitless love, God seeks us the way a shepherd seeks a lost sheep.

God's love has made me realise that while my daughters are different in both the way they think and the way they behave (which is not always good), I can still love them. I will always care for them, bring them up and teach them. The rest I leave with God.

Prayer: *O God, thank you for your eternal love. Help us follow your example by loving others. Make us loving brothers and sisters as we pray, 'Our Father in heaven, hallowed be your name, your kingdom come, your will be done on earth as it is in heaven. Give us today our daily bread. Forgive us our debts, as we also have forgiven our debtors. And lead us not into temptation, but deliver us from the evil one.'* Amen*

Thought for the Day: As different as we are, God loves us all the same.

Wipapan Nangsomboon (Chiang Mai Province, Thailand)

PRAYER FOCUS: PARENTS

* Matthew 6:9–13 (NIV)

No Amen, Yet

Read James 5:13–16
Pray without ceasing.
1 Thessalonians 5:17 (NRSV)

When I was a little girl, I lived two houses away from my grandmother and spent much time following her around. The dark brown cabinets and table in her kitchen represented warmth and security to me. When life wasn't treating me fairly, Grandmother soothed my wounded heart with peanut butter sandwiches and stories about her childhood.

For as long as I can remember, my grandmother has walked with assistance—at one time with a stick and now with a walking frame. My young girl's prayers were for my grandmother to be able to run again. Daily I prayed that Grandmother's legs would become stronger. One afternoon as I watched her walk with her typical step-and-hop, my heart reached out to her. 'Grandmother,' I said, 'I'm praying for your legs, and I haven't said amen yet.' I had learned the verse about praying without ceasing in my Sunday school class, and for me as a child that meant praying without saying amen.

Our family has laughed over that story for years. But the simple truth is, we should always pray with that attitude. Prayer can be a continual conversation with God. God is a friend we can speak with all day, a close companion who wants to listen to the stories of our heart.

Prayer: *Dear heavenly Father, thank you for the privilege of prayer. Help us to pray continually, for we know you hear all of our prayers. Amen*

Thought for the Day: Prayer is a never-ending conversation with God.

Carol Hatcher (Georgia)

The Best Gift

Read Luke 2:1–7

To you is born this day in the city of David a Saviour, who is the Messiah, the Lord.

Luke 2:11 (NRSV)

My husband works hard in a normally well-paying job. One Christmas season, we looked forward to a dinner table full of food and lots of gifts under the Christmas tree. Instead, at the end of the working week, my husband received his cheque only to learn that it was impossible to cash because there were no funds in the company's account.

Our Christmas Eve dinner was meagre. The earnings from that cheque would have seen us through for the remainder of the month. Instead, we had to be very careful how we used the little money we had left.

After dinner, I sat my children around me and told them again the story of Jesus' birth. On that night long ago, the baby Jesus wrapped in swaddling clothes and lying in a manger was the most precious gift of all. I went on to tell them that Jesus Christ was God become human and brought us God's teachings and salvation. Then we sang carols. Our home was filled with joy.

It was the most wonderful Christmas I've ever had because we set aside all insignificant things and allowed the true meaning of Christmas to surface. On that memorable night, it was as if we had been transported to Bethlehem to be with the shepherds. Our hearts were overflowing with happiness.

Prayer: *Thank you, Lord, for the best gift of all, Jesus Christ, who brings us light and love today and every day. Amen*

Thought for the Day: The priceless truth of Christmas is not found in what we can buy.

Neri Gattinoni (Buenos Aires, Argentina)

PRAYER FOCUS: THOSE WHO HAVE NOT HEARD THE GOOD NEWS 123

Jesus at the Disco

Read Mark 1:35–39

Jesus said, 'Let us go somewhere else—to the nearby villages—so I can preach there also. That is why I have come.'
Mark 1:38 (NIV)

Over the last ten years I have conducted Christmas Eve services in some unlikely places—restaurants, fire-stations, football-stadium car parks and prisons. On Christmas Eve two years ago, I participated as over 350 people, nearly all strangers to one another, gathered for a Christmas Eve service of carols, candlelight and communion—in a disco and bar in the town centre. In this unlikely venue, I saw God move in the hearts and lives of people, most of whom never would have stepped through the door of a church. It was a powerful reminder to me that in Jesus, God reveals the intention to encounter us where we are.

Many times those of us in the church forget that Jesus was not born in a church or cathedral; he was born in the dirt and dung of a stable for animals. He was born in the midst of the reality of life, not as in some stained-glass portrayal of a royal birth. This was a real God, for real people, in real life. That's what Emmanuel, 'God with us', means.

The true miracle of Christmas is not found in the pageantry of a great Christmas Eve service. The true miracle of Christmas is the truth that God is with us in the dirt and 'dailyness', and in the reality and imperfection of our lives.

Prayer: *O God, thank you that we do not have to be perfect to welcome you. We give thanks for the miracle of your coming to us. Amen*

Thought for the Day: Christmas is not as much about us coming to God as about God coming to us where we are, as we are.

Mack Strange (Tennessee)

Life Stories

Read John 1:1–18

'The thief comes only to steal and kill and destroy. I came that they may have life, and have it abundantly.'
John 10:10 (NRSV)

My mother lives about 550 miles away. When I phone her, one of the first things she likes to tell me about is what she has read in *The Upper Room* that day. 'Let me read this to you.' And she does. Then she says, 'Don't you love the stories people tell? They are so real. I think it's wonderful how they find that God is with them and that they can put themselves into God's hands—whatever is happening.'

In the Bible as well as in *The Upper Room*, we read stories of Jesus' presence in family matters, relationships, commerce, sickness, injustice and everyday matters such as looking for lost coins and baking bread. So we have stories about him then and now, stories of people entrusting themselves into God's care. These stories link our lives with God, and we too are encouraged to put ourselves into God's hands, whatever is going on.

Jesus—Emmanuel, 'God with us'—shows us how to be human. Starting with his vulnerable infancy, we don't see him 'saving souls' so much as entering into, living with and saving our humanity by inviting us into the hands of God, hands that lovingly shape us into who we are created to be. God's promise is nothing less than life in all of its fullness and, fully alive, we glorify the One who is always with us. And that's another good story.

Prayer: *Thank you, loving God, for Jesus, the way, the truth and the life of our humanity. In him, may we live our lives to the full and glorify you. Amen*

Thought for the Day: Jesus is our picture of what it means to be fully alive.

John Franklin (Manawatu, New Zealand)

PRAYER FOCUS: FAMILIES SEPARATED AT CHRISTMAS

After Christmas

Read Esther 9:18–23

If you offer your food to the hungry and satisfy the needs of the afflicted, then your light shall rise in the darkness.
Isaiah 58:10 (NRSV)

Esther's people set aside two days of celebration that would later become the Festival of Purim. They marked the moment when they were delivered from their enemies, when their sorrow was turned into gladness and their mourning into holiday. They gave presents and food to one another, including the poor. No one was left out of the celebration.

But I wonder how the poor felt when the party was over. Did God's people choose to continue looking after them, or did everything go back to normal, and the poor remain the poor—out there on their own?

At times the plight of the poor comes into the spotlight in national or international emergencies, and practical giving increases sharply as people respond with what they have. But the media circus moves on, or the celebration ends and the holidays are over—and the needs of the poor slip out of our view. The stuff of our daily life preoccupies us. Yet scripture tells us that responding to the needs of the poor is to be part of serving God all through the year.

Prayer: *Lord Jesus, help us to make the needs of others a daily priority and work to relieve suffering. Help us to see your face in the needy and reach out to them as if we are reaching out to you. Amen*

Thought for the Day: If we say we love God, we have to care for God's children.

Susan Hibbins (England)

Rest

Read Psalm 23
Jesus said, 'Come to me, all you who are weary and burdened, and I will give you rest.'
Matthew 11:28 (NIV)

Outside my front window, the branches of the pine trees sagged toward the ground from the weight of ice left by wintry weather. Over the next few hours, I watched as many of the branches snapped and fell. As I watched them break, I felt I too might break from a stressful load I'd been carrying. The suicide of a friend had left me with the weight of many unanswered questions.

But I began to sense God speaking to me: the answer for the trees and for me was warmth. The sun's warmth eventually melted the ice and relieved the trees of their burden. Likewise, instead of continuing to wrestle with all the heavy questions, I began to surrender them to God and to dwell on the warmth of God's love for me.

As I changed my focus from the constant 'whys', my burden began to melt away and I once more experienced peace. It has been many years since my friend's death, and almost all of the questions I asked still remain unanswered, but I rest in the reality of God's unchanging love.

Prayer: *Dear Lord, thank you for your offer of abundant rest if we come to you. We surrender our burdens to you now. Amen*

Thought for the Day: In the face of all our questions, we can rest in the warmth of God's love.

Link2Life: *Volunteer for a counselling help-line in your area.*

Beverly Varnado (Georgia)

PRAYER FOCUS: FAMILIES OF THOSE WHO HAVE TAKEN THEIR OWN LIVES   127

Who Leads?

Read 1 Corinthians 3:4–9

The one who plants and the one who waters really do not matter. It is God who matters, because he makes the plant grow.
1 Corinthians 3:7 (GNB)

While attending a Christian conference, my friend and I were introduced to a young man who was eager to know God. The conference leader asked if we could explain the gospel to him and show him how to become a Christian. We talked with him about the Bible's message of salvation, answered his questions and then led him in a prayer to receive Christ. My friend and I were overjoyed that we had played a part in introducing him to Christ.

We had just met this young man, but God had been drawing him toward relationship with Christ long before that day. He may have read about God or heard others speak about the Lord. Perhaps other people had talked to him about God and prayed for him. His meeting with my friend and me was a step in his journey, and others would come after us to help him grow in faith.

Whatever our part in helping others to come to Christ, we can remember that God is the one who draws them close and makes them grow. What a privilege it is to join the Lord in that work!

Prayer: *Dear God, thank you for drawing people to you and for letting us work with you, no matter what part we play in helping people know you. Amen*

Thought for the Day: How can I work with God to bring people to Christ?

Nola Passmore (Queensland, Australia)

Just Sow

Read 2 Corinthians 9:6–12

Now to [God] who by the power at work within us is able to accomplish far more than we can ask or imagine, to him be glory.
Ephesians 3:20–21 (NRSV)

I work in a large, well-respected hospital. Last week I met Sister Emmanuel, the woman who was sent to our town in the early 1970s to oversee construction of our building. I wanted to show her the many wards and clinics, pointing out how grand the work she began has become. She wasn't interested. It's not that she doesn't care; she simply was more interested in telling me of her work among the poor in Taiwan, in Thailand, in Angola, in rural Mississippi.

Sister Emmanuel helped me to see that we err when we measure success by focusing on outcomes. Life seldom unfolds as we plan, and faith tells us that our lives are part of the ever-unfolding work of God. In this light, success is less about outcomes than about the integrity and enthusiasm of our efforts. All we do is sow seed with purpose. Placed in God's care, these seeds take root, growing and bearing fruit that others will reap —just as our patients reap healing and many good gifts growing from seeds sown by Sister Emmanuel and others.

We can take courage from remembering that God takes our efforts and blesses them, bringing results far richer than anything we can possibly imagine—and certainly far beyond any specific outcome we might expect.

Prayer: *Generous God, thank you for those whose efforts bless our days. Help us to sow seeds of your goodness for those who come after us, leaving outcomes with you. Amen*

Thought for the Day: God brings abundant fruit from the seeds of caring we plant.

Jerry Kearney (Tennessee)

Ugly Bulbs

Read 1 Corinthians 15:35–38, 51–57
What you sow does not come to life unless it dies.
1 Corinthians 15:36 (NRSV)

'What an odd gift to bring to a grieving widow,' I thought as I opened the white box a choir member had brought me. Inside were a dozen shrivelled, brown bulbs.

She explained, 'When our son died several years ago, a friend brought us tulip bulbs to plant. When they bloomed, we were to remember the resurrection. I wanted to do the same for you.'

I enlisted the help of a friend to plant the bulbs. In the grey, dreary weather of November, we planted those ugly, brown bulbs in the border around the patio where my green-fingered husband had raised many lovely flowers. When spring came, there they were—red and yellow tulips bursting with life and beauty.

I was reminded of 1 Corinthians. As the seed must die in order to become a living plant, we too must die in order to enter fully the kingdom of eternal life. That spring I enjoyed the tulips and thanked God for the promise of resurrection.

Prayer: *Loving God, help us not to despair but to find comfort in the many ways you come to us. Amen*

Thought for the Day: In times of grief, God reminds us of the hope we have in Jesus' resurrection.

Sally Woodard (West Virginia)

New Year's Resolution

Read Colossians 3:1–17

Whatever you do, in word or deed, do everything in the name of the Lord Jesus.

Colossians 3:17 (NRSV)

As the New Year rolls in, I am wondering about my New Year's resolutions—all the things I want to accomplish. But as I think about what my resolutions might be, somehow I want to do more than write them down, knowing that in a month or so they will become merely ink on a piece of paper.

Then, I found my answer in Colossians 3:1–17: this year and every year, my resolutions should focus not on me and what will make me look better but on Christ and the place I give him in my life. Are my eyes fixed on myself or on Christ? When people look at me, do they see Christ's compassion, kindness, humility, gentleness and patience? Or do they see my anger, lack of compassion and lack of forgiveness?

In this new year I want the light of Christ in me to shine brightly. I want to show those who have strayed, those who don't know Christ, those who are tired and looking for true peace, joy, and happiness that they can find what they need in Christ. This is my resolution.

Prayer: *Dear heavenly Father, show us how to set our heart, eyes and mind on you. Let your light of love shine through us. In Jesus' name. Amen*

Thought for the Day: What are my spiritual resolutions for the new year?

Wendy Garner (Texas)

Small Group Questions

Wednesday 1 September

1. Is it wrong to help people when we don't really feel like doing so? Is service less valuable depending on our attitude while we serve? Why do you say this?

2. 2 Corinthians 1:3–5 tells us to pass along the 'comfort wherewith we… have been comforted by God'. How do we experience God's comfort? How can we offer it to others? What interferes with experiencing the comfort God offers?

3. How has a serious loss affected your life? Do we ever really 'get over' tragic loss? If not, what makes you say so? If so, how does this come about?

4. As time passes, do you feel that you are becoming more or less compassionate and willing to help others? Why?

5. Describe both a time when you were 'a person in need' and a time when you were 'a person who needed to help'. What did you learn from these experiences?

6. Relate a time when God used a life situation to help you examine yourself.

Wednesday 8 September

1. What is the smallest matter you have ever prayed about? (Be honest!) Was that prayer answered? If so, how? If not, did it change the way you pray?

2. What is the most important matter you have ever prayed about? Was that prayer answered? If so, how? If not, did it change the way you pray?

3. When have you experienced something like Mary Dess did? Do you think God actually 'stretches' people's resources so they can help others?

4. Do you think God responds in different ways to prayers about some matters and to prayers about other matters? What would make a difference to God?

5. Do you agree that God welcomes all our prayers, all the time? If not, what might we pray for that would displease God?

6. Do you believe what Jesus said, 'Whatever you ask for in prayer with faith, you will receive' (Matthew 21:22)? Why or why not?

Wednesday 15 September

1. Bayu Probo's experience sounds very familiar, as if it could happen to thousands of people in the United States or Britain or China or Australia—as well as in Indonesia. What does this say to you about international and cultural differences and likenesses? In a similar situation, do you think you'd feel as Bayu did?

2. By praying for his new city, Bayu gains the satisfaction of obeying God and the city benefits from his petitions. What other benefits does this practice offer?

3. Whom do you know who has lost a job and is looking for work? What does this feel like or do you imagine it feels like? How might or does this experience test our faith?

4. What gifts come with having new people on the job, in the church, and in your neighbourhood?

5. How do you incorporate prayer into your ordinary activities? What sights move you to pray?

6. Describe a time when you felt as if you had been 'sent into exile'. What helped you at that time to cope with the situation?

7. How does your congregation respond to newcomers, especially those from other cultures? How could you be more welcoming to these people?

Wednesday 22 September

1. Do you experience inner nudges that you recognise as coming from God? If so, how do you distinguish between these nudges and your own ideas? Does God have a distinctive 'voice' (figuratively speaking) for you?

2. If you do not receive inner nudges, how do you usually perceive God's guidance? Does God speak to you through scripture? Through sermons? Through books? Through those close to you? How can we know when God is 'speaking' to us?

3. How can we help people trust us to listen and to care about their struggles? How can we serve God by listening to a friend?

4. Thinking back over the meditations you've read in The Upper Room, did some seem to be written especially for you the very day you read them? Why do you say this? How do you see God's hand at work in such situations?

5. What most often keeps you from listening to those in need? Will you do anything differently because of discussing this meditation? If so, what? If not, why not?

6. How good are you at drawing out your friends to discover the ways they might need your help? What method(s) do you use?

7. Do you let your friends and family know when you are in the midst of a particular trial or crisis? If not, why not? If so, how easy is this for you? Why?

Wednesday 29 September

1. What do you think it would feel like to be enfolded in God's arms? What images come to mind when you consider this?

2. Where is the line between feeling comforted by God and needing the presence of a human touch? Is spiritual comfort enough for you, or do you need literal arms around you?

3. Why do some of us seem to experience God's presence when we are in extreme situations in a way that we do not otherwise?

4. How can we help grieving people to come into God's comforting presence?

5. Describe in your own words what 'rich and abundant love' means.

6. Ivelina never thought she would live alone, without her dear husband. Have you thought about which crises or losses you might expect to face and which you would never expect? What determines which situation goes in which category?

7. Have you ever sought help from God by just reading the first page(s) in the Bible that you come to? Was it helpful? How do you feel about this approach?

Wednesday 6 October

1. What recent scandal or public gaffe has caused you to think of someone in a less positive way than before it happened? How many such incidents can you list? What do these say to you about human nature?

2. What is the last thing you said that you would not want repeated? (Paraphrase if necessary.) What action do you need to take in connection with what you said?

3. If you were this writer, what would you say to the criticised orchestra member when you went back to rehearsal? Have you ever had to make such a speech? If so, how was it received?

4. How could Christians be convicted/guilty of hypocrisy? What are some possible effects of hypocrisy within the community of faith?

5. What does the Bible say about the tongue and how we are to speak to one another? About one another? When we are tempted to criticise or make an unkind comment about someone, what could help us to be more gracious?

6. Do you struggle more with what you say or what you do? Why is this?

7. We know that God sets up standards for what we say and do. Does what we think also matter to God? Support your answer.

Wednesday 13 October

1. How can we distinguish between keeping busy in a positive way and hiding/running from negative feelings? Is it ever good to deny our feelings? Why or why not?

2. How does your congregation recognise those who serve in it? Should you do more to recognise them?

3. What song(s) do you sing or listen to, to help you remember or focus on God's presence and power? Which words or phrases elicit a response from you?

4. Who has brought you 'a song in the night' when you were going through a difficult time?

5. What do you think of Deanna Overstreet's advice that using our talents and skills to help someone else can also help us when we are grieving?

6. What creative abilities would you add to Deanna's list? What/who made you think of these additions?

7. Which of your talents/skills came to mind when you read this meditation? When was the last time you used this skill to serve others? What is the most unusual talent you've seen used in ministry?

Wednesday 20 October

1. How do you pray differently now from when you first began to pray? Do you pray the Lord's Prayer daily or fairly often? Why or why not?

2. How might this writer's attitude toward prayer be different if her Sunday school teacher had not recovered?

3. This meditation almost equates prayer with intercession. What other kinds of prayer are there? Which of these do you most often pray?

4. Describe the first time you can remember having 'a dialogue with God'. If you have never 'talked' with God, what prevents you from doing so?

5. At what age should we start teaching children to pray? How does/should our approach differ as they age?

6. How can teaching about prayer address times when God doesn't appear to answer our prayers? At what point should we address this issue?

Wednesday 27 October

1. Who was the biggest influence on you in your teenage years? Was the influence positive or negative? At what age did you feel most vulnerable to peer pressure? What influences do teenagers face these days that you did not have to contend with?

2. According to today's writer, negativity, gossip, prejudice and greed can all be contagious. What 'carriers' of these do you encounter often? How can we immunise ourselves against 'catching' these and other unhelpful behaviour?

3. Consider your interactions with friends, neighbours or colleagues. Do you tend to rub off on them, or are they rubbing off on you? How so?

4. Can you think of people whose lives have been changed—for better or worse—because of the company they keep/kept?

5. How has peer pressure changed from when you were a child to now that you are an adult? At which stage did you feel most vulnerable?

6. How can we be aware of the difference between keeping ourselves 'unstained by the world' and isolating ourselves from others, appearing aloof or self-righteous?

Wednesday 3 November

1. Does this meditation make you feel either guilty or proud? Why or why not?

2. Is frugality a Christian virtue or value? What passages of scripture support your answer?

3. Do you think most people give out of gratitude or out of guilt? Does it matter, as long as they give?

4. John Wesley taught, 'Earn all you can; give all you can; save all you can.' Which of these do you do best? How does our culture support or discourage each one of these actions?

5. How does your church support simple living? Does your church support 'alternative giving' at Christmas? Should it?

6. Rebecca admits to what she seems to think is excessive affection for books and magazines. How did you respond to that part of her meditation? What non-essentials or 'extras' do you spend money on regularly? Is it easy or difficult for you to answer that last question?

7. Jesus states in Luke 12:34: 'Where your treasure is, there your heart will be also.' Where has your heart been that it shouldn't be?

8. In John Wesley's class meetings (small discipleship groups), members reported each week how much they had given to the church and how much they had given to the poor. How would people in your congregation respond if this were suggested for members? Required of them?

Wednesday 10 November

1. Who has inspired you to want to know more about the Bible? How did they do this?

2. Do you know someone like Gail? If so, what did you learn from that person? Are you such a person? If not, would you want to be?

3. If you were grading yourself (A-B-C-D-E) on your recent attention to scripture, what would your grade be? What evidence supports your evaluation?

4. How many Bibles do you own? Which one do you treasure most, and why? Which translation of the Bible is your favourite for daily/ devotional reading? Why?

5. 'The word of God is living and active' (Hebrews 4:12). Does this mean that it is dynamic, that it can change with the culture or the time? If so, give a support for this conclusion from scripture. If not, what do you think the writer of Hebrews means by this description?

6. Paul states that scripture is 'useful for teaching, rebuking, correcting and training in righteousness' (2 Timothy 3:16). When have you used it for any of these purposes?

7. What does 'spiritual power' mean to you? How might one find/ receive spiritual power?

Wednesday 17 November

1. When was the last time (if ever) someone asked you to pray for them? Did you? What difference does it make whether we pray for others or not?

2. Some people think that good Christian parents and families never or rarely have problems with addiction. In your experience, is this true? Why might people think it is true?

3. Some people are like the Trudels, talking openly about struggles in their family; others keep such situations private. If someone in your family had a drug problem, which approach would you take, and why?

4. What addictions are acceptable in our culture? Are some addictions positive? If so, which ones? If not, why do you say this?

5. Whom would you ask to pray for you about your most serious struggles? Why would you choose this (these) person(s)?

6. This family's struggle went on for years. What are the special challenges in praying for people with long-term needs? When are we called to do more than 'just pray'?

7. Paul tells us, 'In everything, by prayer and petition, with thanksgiving, present your requests to God' (Philippians 4:5–6). Do you do this? What do you have trouble presenting? Why?

Wednesday 24 November

1. When was the last time you 'played'? What did you do? Were you with a child, or alone? Is playing a natural behaviour or a learned one? Why do you say this?

2. How do you respond to pictures of Darfur or other faraway places where people are in dire need? How did you respond to the pictures of New Orleans after Hurricane Katrina or pictures of Haiti after the 2010 earthquake? Is there a difference in how we respond to suffering far away and suffering close at hand? Should there be?

3. What refugees are mentioned in the Bible? How are God's people told to respond to them? What lessons can we learn from their stories?

4. Paul directs us to 'give thanks in all circumstances' (1 Thessalonians 5:18). Are there any circumstances in which you find it very hard to give thanks? When have you begrudgingly given thanks for a trying circumstance and then later realised that circumstance to be a blessing?

5. What is your faith community doing to help desperate refugees and struggling people all over the world? What more could you do?

6. What 'small joys in life' do you delight in often? How do you express your thankfulness?

7. What can you do to teach young children about the peace that comes from a grateful attitude?

Wednesday 1 December

1. In your household, who is in charge of decorating for Christmas? Is decorating a family ritual? If so, when and how is it done? Or, if you do not decorate, in what special ways do you celebrate this season?

2. How do you feel about graveyards? How do you respond to this image of a Christmas tree in a graveyard?

3. What is your favourite aspect of celebrating Christmas? Is your answer different now from what it would have been 10 or 15 years ago? Why or why not?

4. Why do losses seem especially poignant at holiday times? Have you ever suffered a great loss just before a holiday? If so, how did it affect your response to the holiday that year? In later years?

5. Whom do you know who has recently had a loved one die? How can you support this person/these persons as Christmas approaches?

6. What special service of healing or hope does your church offer at this time of year? If there are none, how might you support your church in beginning one?

7. Should Christians celebrate Christmas differently from non-Christians? What parts of your celebration are secular? What is specifically Christian about the way you celebrate Christmas?

8. How does Christ 'offer comfort to the broken-hearted and hope to the lonely'?

Wednesday 8 December

1. What do you think this writer means by 'celebrate this Christmas well'? What constitutes celebrating well versus celebrating badly?

2. Do people in your town and/or family visit graves at particular times of year? If so, what is done during these visits? If not, how does the idea of such visiting affect you?

3. When has celebrating a holiday brought you to a spiritual decision or spiritual healing? How did this come about?

4. To whom do you need to give the gift of forgiveness this Christmas? Are you ready to do it, or will you wait until another year? What passages from the Bible indicate that you should do it now?

5. What struggle from your past do you want to put to rest this year? What steps will you take to do so? How do you want group members to pray for you about this?

6. Our quoted scripture mentions, 'forgetting what is behind' (Philippians 3:13). Does this apply in all circumstances? When should we forget about the events of the past and when should we remember them?

7. What relationship in your life has been difficult? Why? What do you think could help mend this relationship?

Wednesday 15 December

1. Do you have a memory of being left out when you were young? If so, what is it? Do you think most people have a similar memory? If so, why? If not, why not?

2. What memories of being included are special to you from your school years? Who was your best friend when you were at school? Are you still in touch with this person?

3. What does this meditation say to you about human nature? What spiritual truth do you see in Ronald's experience?

4. Some people say that the church should be a place that especially welcomes those the world shoves aside. Is your church like that—a variety of people some of whom would not be considered 'nice' or 'successful' in the world's eyes? Would Jesus feel welcome in your congregation on an average Sunday morning?

5. How does your church reach out to the community to help people who are sometimes not welcome—people facing addiction, financial ruin, or mental or emotional problems? Do you think Jesus would reach out to these people if he lived in your neighbourhood?

6. How has Jesus made you feel chosen and welcome?

7. What characteristic or trait makes you unique? Which characteristics or traits do you think are significant to God?

8. In our reading for today, Jesus says, 'This is my command: love each other' (John 15:17). Is this a command we can obey? How can love be legislated? How does this verse reveal that God's definition of love may differ greatly from the world's?

Wednesday 22 December

1. Who was your favourite family member or adult friend when you were a child? Why and how did you become attached to this person? What did you learn from the relationship? How can you see its influence in your life today?

2. Whom do you know who has physical limitations and yet lives as a positive witness for God? What life lessons can you draw from this person's example?

3. Carol assumed that God wanted her grandmother to be healed. How do you feel about the reality that some people are not healed even though we pray for it? Can we pray with the same attitude that Carol had as a child? Why or why not?

4. For what or whom have you been praying for a long time? Are you ever tempted to give up? If so, why do you keep on praying? If not, what sustains you in praying?

5. How can we 'pray without ceasing'? What ways of praying have been helpful for you?

6. What is your favourite Bible story or Bible verse about prayer? Why is it a favourite?

7. How is prayer essential to faith?

Wednesday 29 December

1. If you were Jerry, how might Sister Emmanuel's lack of interest in seeing the hospital affect you? Was her attitude Christian or not? What makes you say this?

2. Who in your community has worked hard from Christian motives to improve your town? What can you do to let them know you appreciate what they have done?

3. Whom do you know who works in health care as a God-given calling? How is this person's work different from those with different motives?

4. Do you agree that success is more about 'integrity and enthusiasm' than about outcomes? Does our culture agree with Jerry's assessment?

5. How do you measure success or achievement in someone's life? In your own life? How might that differ from God's perspective?

6. Does your church place more emphasis on worship or outreach? What qualifies your answer?

7. How has your life been 'part of the ever-unfolding work of God'?

8. Read aloud Jeremiah 29:5–7. What does this passage say to you about how God's people are to live? What parallels 'building houses'? What parallels 'planting trees'? What parallels 'seek the welfare of the city'? How do you pray for your city? What are the special needs of your community, and how can you serve God in meeting them?

Bible Reading Resources Pack

A pack of resources and ideas to help to promote Bible reading in your church is available from BRF. The pack, which will be of use at any time during the year (but especially for Bible Sunday in October), includes sample readings from BRF's Bible reading notes and The People's Bible Commentary, a sermon outline, an all-age sketch, a children's activity, information about BRF's ministry and much more.

Unless you specify the month in which you would like the pack sent, we will send it immediately on receipt of your order. We greatly appreciate your donations towards the cost of producing the pack (without them we would not be able to make the pack available) and we welcome your comments about the contents of the pack and your ideas for future ones.

This coupon should be sent to:
BRF, 15 The Chambers, Vineyard, Abingdon OX14 3FE

Name..

Address ....

....Postcode..

Telephone ....

Email...

Please send me...................................Bible Reading Resources Pack(s).

Please send the pack now/ in ....(month).

I enclose a donation for £ .... towards the cost of the pack.

BRF is a Registered Charity

Subscriptions

The Upper Room is published in January, May and September.

Individual subscriptions

The subscription rate for orders for 4 or fewer copies includes postage and packing: THE UPPER ROOM annual individual subscription   £13.50

Church subscriptions

Orders for 5 copies or more, sent to ONE address, are post free:
THE UPPER ROOM annual church subscription   £10.50

Please do not send payment with order for a church subscription. We will send an invoice with your first order.

Please note that the annual billing period for church subscriptions runs from 1 May to 30 April.

Copies of the notes may also be obtained from Christian bookshops.

Single copies of *The Upper Room* will cost £3.50. Prices valid until 30 April 2011.

Individual Subscriptions

☐ I would like to take out a subscription myself (complete your name and address details only once)

☐ I would like to give a gift subscription (please complete both name and address sections below)

Your name...

Your address..

....Postcode..................................

Gift subscription name..

Gift subscription address...

....Postcode..................................

Gift message (20 words max)...

....

Please send *The Upper Room* beginning with the January 2011 issue:

THE UPPER ROOM ☐ £13.50

Please complete the payment details below and send, with appropriate payment, to:
BRF, 15 The Chambers, Vineyard, Abingdon OX14 3FE

Total enclosed £.......... (cheques should be made payable to 'BRF')

Payment by ☐ cheque ☐ postal order ☐ Visa ☐ Mastercard ☐ Switch

Card no: | | | | | | | | | | | | | | | | | | |

Expires: | | | | Security code: | | |

Issue no (Switch): | | | |

Signature (essential if paying by credit/Switch card) ....

☐ Please do not send me further information about BRF publications

☐ Please send me a Bible reading resources pack to encourage Bible reading in my church

BRF is a Registered Charity

Church Subscriptions

☐ Please send me ...... copies of *The Upper Room* September 2010 / January / May 2011 issue (delete as applicable)

Name..

Address ....

....Postcode.....................................

Telephone ....

Email...

Please send this completed form to:
BRF, 15 The Chambers, Vineyard, Abingdon OX14 3FE

Please do not send payment with this order. We will send an invoice with your first order.

Christian bookshops: All good Christian bookshops stock BRF publications. For your nearest stockist, please contact BRF.

Telephone: The BRF office is open between 09.15 and 17.30. To place your order, telephone 01865 319700; fax 01865 319701.

Web: Visit www.brf.org.uk

☐ Please send me a Bible reading resources pack to encourage Bible reading in my church

BRF is a Registered Charity

UR0310

Pilgrims to the Manger

Exploring the wonder of God with us

Naomi Starkey

This book is an invitation to a pilgrimage through Advent, to Christmas itself and on to Epiphany. As the days and weeks pass, we will reflect on a range of issues—the significance of the festivities, the values that underpin our lives, some of the other special days in the Church calendar at this time, and how we can begin to deepen our understanding of God's perspective on our world, our church and ourselves.

'Pilgrimage' is more than a figure of speech in this book, however. You are invited to join an imaginary group of pilgrims on a path that starts in an average high street and leads through and beyond the city, offering lessons from the sights and sounds encountered along the way. It's not a conventional pilgrimage, following a well-trodden route to a well-known destination, but it is a pilgrimage of both head and heart that will help us to explore something of what it means to say that God is with us. We will see, too, how this truth brings both challenge and consolation for us as we follow the Christ-child.

ISBN 978 1 84101 709 9   £7.99
To order a copy of this book, please turn to the order form on page 157.

Celebrating the King James Version

Devotional readings from the classic translation

Rachel Boulding

This book of Bible readings and reflections has been published as part of the celebrations for the 400th anniversary of a classic Bible translation, first published in 1611 yet still widely used and loved around the world today. The King James Version (also known as the Authorised Version) was first published to provide a dignified, authoritative translation for public worship and private prayer, and for centuries it remained the most important Protestant translation into English. It shaped profoundly both English language and literature because of its central place in people's consciousness. At the same time, it offers a unique vision of our relationship with God through the vivid and robust qualities of its expression.

Rachel Boulding's short, insightful devotional readings are drawn from across the King James Version and are written to help the reader reflect on the richness of the language and what it says to us today about faith in God. They can be used for daily reflections, as a bedside book or simply for a fuller appreciation of different parts of the Bible.

The book concludes with an afterword by Professor Alison Shell of Durham University on the cultural and historical significance of this most enduring of Bible translations.

ISBN 978 1 84101 757 0   £9.99   *Available October 2010*
To order a copy of this book, please turn to the order form on page 157.

Bible Word Searches

Jane Butcher

This latest puzzle book from BRF contains 80 word searches, covering a wide variety of Bible-based themes from 'Fruit, vegetables and nuts found in the Bible' to a mini-series of searches covering the events of Christmas. In each of them the words could be hidden horizontally, vertically or diagonally. Some words are written forwards while others may be backwards. The level of challenge ranges from quick and easy to brain-baffling.

Solutions are provided at the back of the book, but for the hardest searches it is up to you to work out which words are included!

ISBN 978 1 84101 789 1   £6.99
To order a copy of this book, please turn to the order form on page 157.

One Dad Encountering God

Brad Lincoln

What if God has left an important clue about his personality some-where inside us, as if, in making us, he left his signature?

This book shares the reflections of one ordinary man about what it means to be a dad—and how that fits in with his feelings about life, the universe and God. If we are made in the image of our heavenly Father, we can learn a lot about what it means to be a dad through looking at what God is like. And reflecting on our relationship with our own children can help us begin to glimpse how God feels about us. *One Dad Encountering God* does not set out to provide all the answers but to get you thinking about what really matters in life.

Includes material for groups.

ISBN 978 1 84101 678 8 £6.99
To order a copy of this book, please turn to the order form on page 157.

Creative Ideas for All-Age Church

12 through-the-year programmes for informal church services and special one-off events

Karen Bulley

The twelve themes in this book contain a wealth of creative worship ideas, all designed to encourage the church family to learn together in worship and grow in faith as part of God's family.

Each theme includes introductory reflections on the season of the year; a biblical context; ideas for a visual display; age-specific activities; suggestions for sharing a meal; suggestions for reflections, prayers and sung worship and, finally, ideas for taking the theme further. The themes can be used to plan stand-alone worship programmes or to follow the pattern of the Christian year, giving an ideal opportunity for a once-a-month exploration of the colour, creativity and individuality of each season.

The material offers a wide range of practical ideas and fun (or reflective) activities designed to give choice to those planning the worship. A pick-and-mix approach provides flexibility for the length and setting of worship.

ISBN 978 1 84101 663 4   £7.99
To order a copy of this book, please turn to the order form on page 157.

Parenting Children for a Life of Faith

Helping children meet and know God

Rachel Turner

Parenting Children for a Life of Faith explores how the home can become the primary place in which children are nurtured into the reality of God's presence and love, equipped to access him themselves and encouraged to grow in a two-way relationship with him that will last a lifetime.

The basic principle behind the ideas explored is that we need to model for our children what it means to be in a relationship with God rather than just equipping them to know about him—helping our children to be God-connected rather than just God-smart.

The material is organised in three parts, which progressively explore:

- Discipling our children proactively
- Modelling the reality of being in a relationship with God
- Tying together truth and experience
- Connecting children to God's heart
- Implementing a plan

ISBN 978 1 84101 607 8   £7.99
To order a copy of this book, please turn to the order form on page 157.

ORDERFORM

REF	TITLE	PRICE	QTY	TOTAL
709 9	Pilgrims to the Manger	£7.99		
757 0	Celebrating the King James Version	£9.99		
789 1	Bible Word Searches	£6.99		
678 8	One Dad Encountering God	£6.99		
663 4	Creative Ideas for All-Age Church	£7.99		
607 8	Parenting Children for a Life of Faith	£7.99		

POSTAGE AND PACKING CHARGES				
Order value	UK	Europe	Surface	Air Mail
£7.00 & under	£1.25	£3.00	£3.50	£5.50
£7.10–£30.00	£2.25	£5.50	£6.50	£10.00
Over £30.00	FREE	prices on request		

Postage and packing	
Donation	
TOTAL	

Name _____ Account Number _____

Address _____

_____ Postcode _____

Telephone Number_____

Email _____

Payment by: ❑ Cheque ❑ Mastercard ❑ Visa ❑ Postal Order ❑ Maestro

Card no ❑❑❑❑ ❑❑❑❑ ❑❑❑❑ ❑❑❑❑ ❑❑❑

Valid from ❑❑❑❑ Expires ❑❑❑❑ Issue no. ❑❑❑

Security code* ❑❑❑ *Last 3 digits on the reverse of the card.
ESSENTIAL IN ORDER TO PROCESS YOUR ORDER

Shaded boxes for
Maestro use only

Signature _____ Date _____

All orders must be accompanied by the appropriate payment.

Please send your completed order form to:
BRF, 15 The Chambers, Vineyard, Abingdon OX14 3FE
Tel. 01865 319700 / Fax. 01865 319701 Email: enquiries@brf.org.uk

❑ Please send me further information about BRF publications.

Available from your local Christian bookshop.   BRF is a Registered Charity

About
brf:

BRF is a registered charity and also a limited company, and has been in existence since 1922. Through all that we do—producing resources, providing training, working face-to-face with adults and children, and via the web—we work to resource individuals and church communities in their Christian discipleship through the Bible, prayer and worship.

Our Barnabas children's team works with primary schools and churches to help children under 11, and the adults who work with them, to explore Christianity creatively and to bring the Bible alive.

To find out more about BRF and its core activities and ministries, visit:

www.brf.org.uk
www.brfonline.org.uk
www.barnabasinschools.org.uk
www.barnabasinchurches.org.uk
www.messychurch.uk
www.foundations21.org.uk

If you have any questions about BRF
and our work, please email us at

enquiries@brf.org.uk

enter